SCOTT FORESMAN ▪ ADDISON WESLEY

Mathematics

Grade 1

Homework Workbook

D1450272

PEARSON

Scott Foresman

Editorial Offices: Glenview, Illinois • Parsippany, New Jersey • New York, New York

Sales Offices: Parsippany, New Jersey • Duluth, Georgia • Glenview, Illinois
Coppell, Texas • Ontario, California • Mesa, Arizona

ISBN 0-328-11687-4

1 2 3 4 5 6 7 8 9 10 V011 09 08 07 06 05 04

Making 6

We can show 6 in different ways.

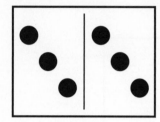 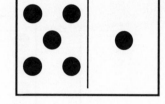

___3___ and ___3___   ___5___ and ___1___

Write the numbers that show ways to make 6.

1.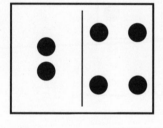

___2___ and ___4___

2.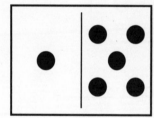

_____ and _____

3.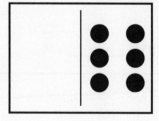

_____ and _____

4.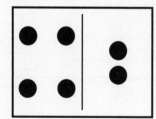

_____ and _____

Name _____

Making 6

We can show 6 in different ways.

Write the numbers that show ways to make 6.

1.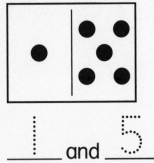

_____ and _____

2.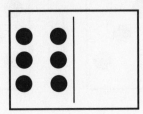

_____ and _____

3.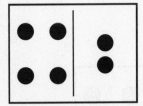

_____ and _____

4.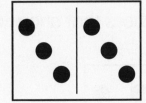

_____ and _____

5.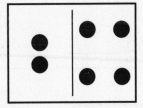

_____ and _____

6.

_____ and _____

Problem Solving *Reasoning*

Solve.

7. Bernie has 3 cats and 2 dogs.
How many pets does he have in all?

_____

© Pearson Education, Inc. 1

Making 7

We can show 7 in different ways.

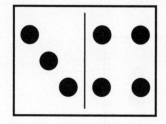 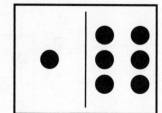

___3___ and ___4___   ___6___ and ___1___

Write the numbers that show ways to make 7.

1.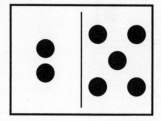

___2___ and ___5___

2.

_____ and _____

3.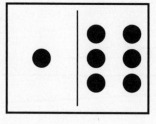

_____ and _____

4.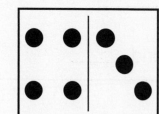

_____ and _____

Name _____

Making 7

We can show 7 in different ways.
Write the numbers that show ways to make 7.

1.
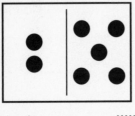
_2_ and _5_

2.

_____ and _____

3.

_____ and _____

4.
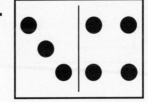
_____ and _____

5.
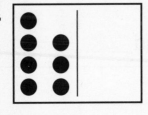
_____ and _____

6.
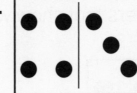
_____ and _____

Problem Solving *Number Sense*

Circle **yes** or **no**.

7. Jill has 5 dots. Can she put the
same number of dots on each hat?

yes   no

Making 8 and 9

We can make 9 in different ways.

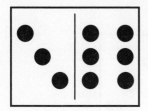 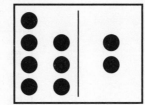 

__3__ and __6__   __7__ and __2__   __1__ and __8__

Write the numbers that show ways to make 8 and 9.

I.

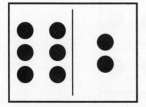

__3__ and __5__

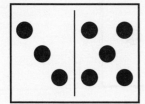

_____ and _____

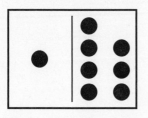

_____ and _____

2.

_____ and _____

_____ and _____

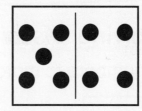

_____ and _____

Making 8 and 9

We can show 8 and 9 in different ways.

Write the numbers that show ways to make 8 and 9.

1.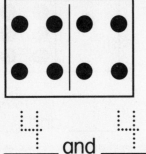

__4__ and __4__

2.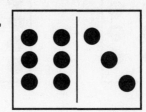

_____ and _____

3.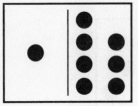

_____ and _____

4.

_____ and _____

5.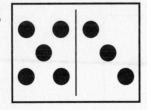

_____ and _____

6.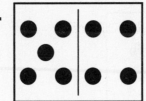

_____ and _____

Problem Solving *Visual Thinking*

7. Write the numbers to match the picture.

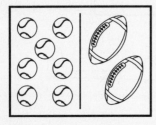

_____ and _____

© Pearson Education, Inc. 1

Making 10

Here are some different ways to make 10.

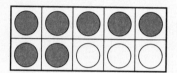

7 and 3

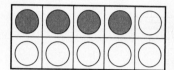

4 and 6

Write the numbers that show ways to make 10.

1.

_6_ and _4_

2.

____ and ____

3.

____ and ____

4.

____ and ____

5.

____ and ____

6.

____ and ____

Making 10

We can show 10 in different ways.

Write the numbers that show ways to make 10.

1.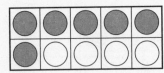

___8___ and ___2___

2.

_____ and _____

3.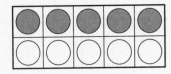

_____ and _____

4.

_____ and _____

5.

_____ and _____

6.

_____ and _____

Problem Solving *Number Sense*

7. Circle all the ways that make 10.

| 4 and 5 | 3 and 7 | 5 and 5 |

| 8 and 2 | 6 and 3 | 2 and 7 |

PROBLEM-SOLVING STRATEGY

Use Objects

What different ways can you put 9 counters on Workmat 1?

> **Read and Understand**

There are 9 counters in all.

> **Plan and Solve**

Put 2 counters on the left part and 7 counters on the right part. Move 1 counter from the right side to the left side. Write the numbers.

> **Look Back and Check**

How do you know your answer is correct?

Workmat 1

1

In All

2	7	9
3		9
		9

Pat wants to put all 9 dots on the clown hats. She wants to put some dots on each hat. Use counters for dots and paper for hats. What other ways can you put 9 dots on 2 clown hats? Write the numbers.

1. __2__ and __7__

2. ____ and ____

Use Objects

In what different ways can you put 6 balls into 2 boxes?
Complete the chart.

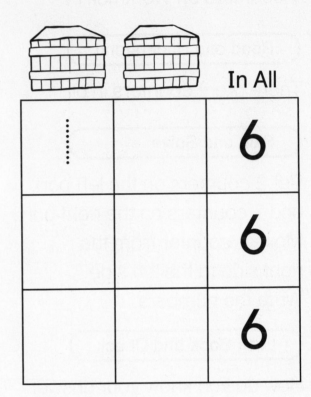

Reasoning *Writing in Math*

Write your own question about
putting some balls into 2 boxes.

_____

_____

_____

1 and 2 More Than

We can find one more than a number.

Count.	Count.	4 and 1 more
There are 4.	There are 5.	4 and 1 more is 5.

We can find two more than a number.

Count.	Count.	4 and 2 more
There are 4.	There are 6.	4 and 2 more is 6.

Use counters to show one and two more.
Write the numbers.

1.

5 and 1 more is _____.   5 and 2 more is _____.

2.

9 and 1 more is _____.   9 and 2 more is _____.

3.    

6 and 2 more is _____.   6 and 1 more is _____.

1 and 2 More Than

Write the numbers.

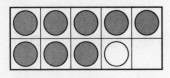

8 and 1 more is __9__.

8 and 2 more is _____.

---

1. 5 and 1 more is _____.

5 and 2 more is _____.

2. 0 and 1 more is _____.

0 and 2 more is _____.

3. 7 and 1 more is _____.

7 and 2 more is _____.

4. 2 and 1 more is _____.

2 and 2 more is _____.

Problem Solving *Algebra*

Write the numbers.

5. 4 and _____ more is 5.

4 and _____ more is 6.

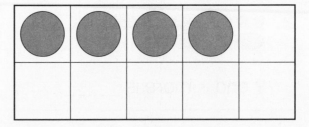

I and 2 Fewer Than

We can find one fewer than a number.

Show 6.	Cross out I.	Now there are 5.

		I fewer than 6 is 5.

We can find two fewer than a number.

Show 4.	Cross out 2.	Now there are 2.

		2 fewer than 4 is 2.

Use counters to show one and two fewer.
Cross out counters. Write the numbers.

1.

   I fewer than 7 is ___6___.

2.

   2 fewer than 8 is _____.

Problem Solving *Algebra*

Use counters to show one and two fewer.
Write the numbers.

3.

   I fewer than _____ is 8.

4.

   2 fewer than _____ is 7.

1 and 2 Fewer Than

Write the numbers.

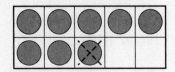

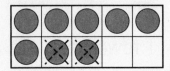

I fewer than 8 is __7__.

2 fewer than 8 is _____.

1. I fewer than 5 is _____. 2 fewer than 5 is _____.	**2.** I fewer than 10 is _____. 2 fewer than 10 is _____.
3. I fewer than 2 is _____. 2 fewer than 2 is _____.	**4.** I fewer than 11 is _____. 2 fewer than 11 is _____.

Problem Solving *Algebra*

Write the numbers.

5. I fewer than _____ is 8.

2 fewer than _____ is 7.

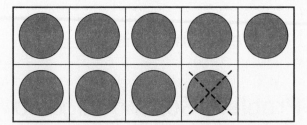

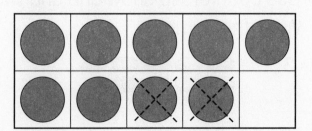

Comparing Numbers to 5 and to 10

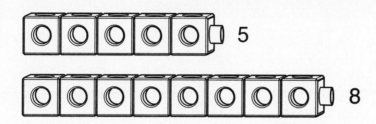 5

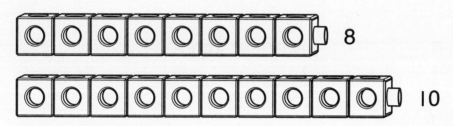 8

8 is more than 5.

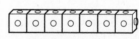 8

10

8 is fewer than 10.

Use cubes. Circle **more** or **fewer**.

I.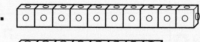

more   fewer

10 is _____ than 7.

2.

more   fewer

5 is _____ than 7.

3.

more   fewer

5 is _____ than 3.

4.

more   fewer

10 is _____ than 8.

Comparing Numbers to 5 and to 10

Circle **fewer** or **more**.

1.

   8 is _____ than 10. (fewer)   more

2.

   2 is _____ than 5.   fewer   more

3.

   7 is _____ than 5.   fewer   more

4.

   12 is _____ than 10.   fewer   more

Problem Solving *Number Sense*

Draw lines to match.

5. **12**   more than 5

    3   more than 10

    7   fewer than 5

Ordering Numbers Through 12

We can put numbers in order.

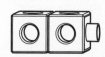 2 is the least.

4

7 is the greatest.

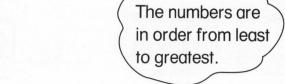

The numbers are in order from least to greatest.

Use cubes. Write the numbers in order from least to greatest.

1. 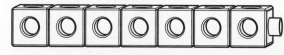 _5_   _3_ is the least.

_3_   _8_ is the greatest.

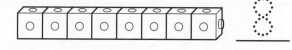 _8_

2. _____   _____ is the least.

_____ is the greatest.

_____

3. _____   _____ is the least.

_____ is the greatest.

_____

Ordering Numbers Through 12

Write the numbers in order from least to greatest.

1.

1, 5, 8
least   greatest

2.

_____, _____, _____
least   greatest

3.

_____, _____, _____
least   greatest

4.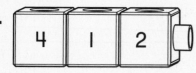

_____, _____, _____
least   greatest

5.

_____, _____, _____
least   greatest

Problem Solving *Reasoning*

6. Kate, Jake, and Matt walk to school.

Kate walks 5 blocks.

Jake walks 3 blocks.

Matt walks 6 blocks.

Who walks the least blocks? _____

Identifying the Pattern Unit

This is a pattern.

  repeats over and over.

This is a pattern, too.

   repeats over and over.

Circle the pattern unit.

1.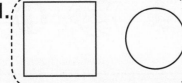

2.

3.

Identifying the Pattern Unit

Circle the pattern unit.

1.

2.

3.

4.

Problem Solving *Algebra*

Circle the shap that does **not** belong in the pattern.

5.

Use with Lesson 1-10.

Look at these patterns.

A   B   A   B   A   B

repeats over and over. AB repeats over and over.

Use pattern blocks. Make a pattern. Draw the pattern.
Then make the same pattern using letters.

I.

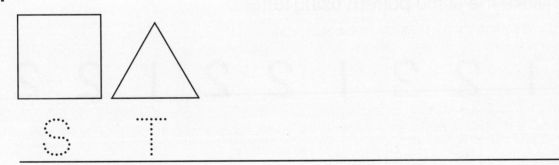

A   B   A   B   A   B

2.

S   T

Translating Patterns

Look at the pattern.
Make the same pattern using letters.

1.

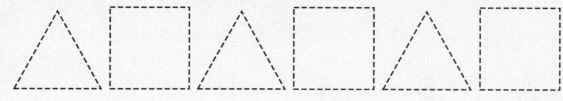

A B A B A B

_____

2.

A B C

_____

Problem Solving *Reasoning*

3. Look at the pattern.
Make the same pattern using letters.

1 2 2 1 2 2 1 2 2

A B B

_____

PROBLEM-SOLVING SKILL

Use Data from a Picture

The stripes make a pattern.
What color should the white stripe be?

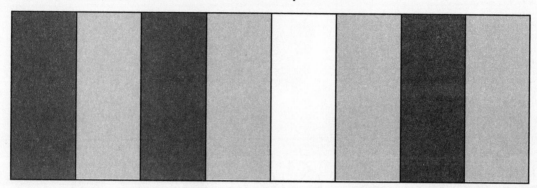

Find the pattern.
Color what is missing.

I.

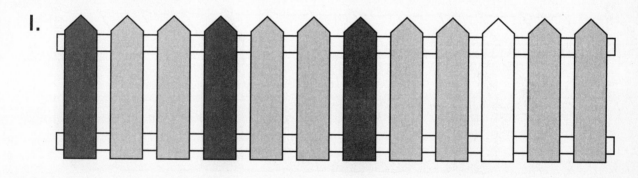

2.

Use Data from a Picture

Find the pattern.
Color what is missing.

1.

2.

3.

Problem Solving *Visual Thinking*

4. Find the pattern.
   Color what is missing.

It's a Party!

This is a pattern. The balloon and party hat repeat over and over.

Find the pattern. Draw what comes next.

1.  _____

2.

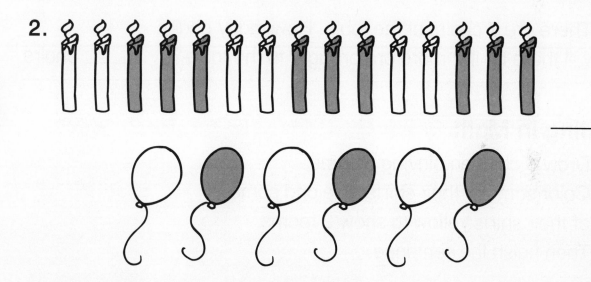 _____

3. How many white balloons are there? _____

4. How many gray balloons are there? _____

5. What color should come next in the pattern? _____

6. If Jeff wants 11 balloons, how many more balloons does he need?

_____ more balloons

It's a Party!

1. Manuel and Dee are setting the table for a party.
Draw what comes next in the pattern.

_____

2. Manuel hangs up 9 party lights. If he hangs up
2 more party lights, how many party lights will
be hanging up?   _____ lights

3. There are 7 chairs at the table. How many chairs
will there be if 2 more are brought to the table?   _____ chairs

Writing in Math

4. Draw 6 children playing a game.
Color some of their shirts blue and some
of their shirts yellow to show 2 teams.
Then finish the sentence.

_____ and _____

Stories About Joining

Join the groups to find how many bugs
there are in all.

Place a counter on each bug. Then count.

2 bugs are on the rock.   3 bugs are on the blanket.

 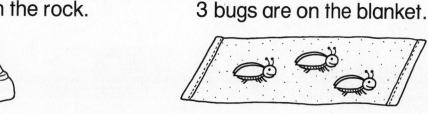

   I   2   3   4   5

How many bugs are there in all? _____ bugs

Tell a joining story for each picture.
Use counters to tell how many in all.

I. 2 birds are in a tree.   2 birds are in a nest.

How many birds are there in all? _____ birds

2. 3 fish are in a bowl.   2 fish are in another bowl.

How many fish are there in all? _____ fish

Stories About Joining

Use counters to answer each question.

1.

4 sheep are in the grass.
4 sheep join them.
How many sheep are there in all? ☐ sheep

2.

6 ducks are swimming.
3 ducks join them.
How many ducks are there in all? ☐ ducks

Problem Solving *Writing in Math*

3. Draw a picture of 4 blue
balloons and 3 red balloons.
Tell how many balloons there are in all.

_____ balloons

Using Counters to Add

Join the parts to make the whole.

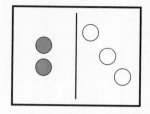

How many black counters? __2__

How many white counters? __3__

 and is _____ in all. 5 is the sum of 2 and 3.

Add to find the sum. Use counters if you like.

1.

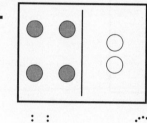

How many black counters? __4__

How many white counters? __2__

_____ and _____ is _____ in all. 6 is the sum of 4 and 2.

2.

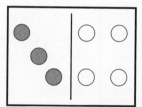

_____ and _____ is _____ in all.

3.

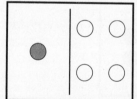

_____ and _____ is _____ in all.

4.

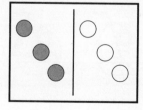

_____ and _____ is _____ in all.

5.

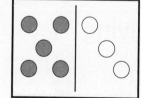

_____ and _____ is _____ in all.

Name _____

Using Counters to Add

Add to find the sum.
Use counters if you like.

1.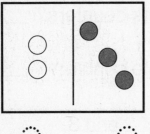

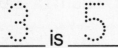
__2__ and __3__ is __5__.

2.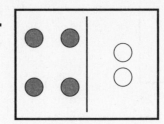

_____ and _____ is _____.

3.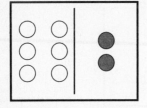

_____ and _____ is _____.

4.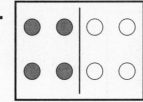

_____ and _____ is _____.

5.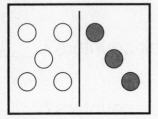

_____ and _____ is _____.

6.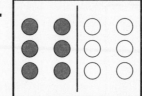

_____ and _____ is _____.

Problem Solving *Reasoning*

7. Is the sum of 3 and 3 more or less than 7? _____

Using Numbers to Add

Find how many in all.

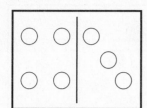

_4_ and _3_ is _7_ in all.

_4_ plus _3_ equals _7_.

4   +   3   =   7

> This is an addition sentence.

Tell how many in all.

Then write an addition sentence.

1.

3 plus 1 equals _4_.

$$3 + 1 = 4$$

2.

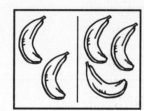

2 plus 3 equals ____.

___ + ___ = ___

3.

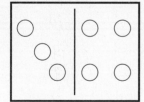

3 plus 4 equals ____.

___ + ___ = ___

4.

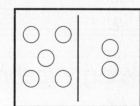

5 plus 2 equals ____.

___ + ___ = ___

Name _____

Using Numbers to Add

Write an addition sentence.

1.

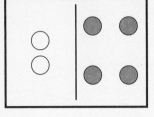

2 + 4 = 6

2.

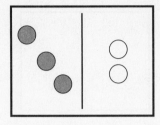

___ + ___ = ___

3.

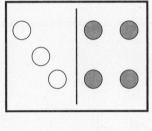

___ + ___ = ___

4.

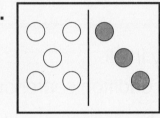

___ + ___ = ___

5.

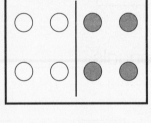

___ + ___ = ___

6.

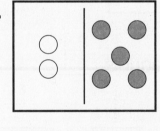

___ + ___ = ___

Problem Solving *Algebra*

7. Ron has 8 caps.

4 of his caps are blue.

The rest of his caps are red.

How many of Ron's caps are red?

_____ red caps

Zero in Addition

How many in each part? How many in all?

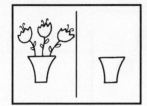

$$3 + 0 = 3$$

$$0 + 4 = 4$$

Write an addition sentence.

1.

$$2 + 0 = 2$$

2.

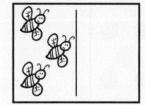

$$\_\_ + 0 = \_\_$$

3.

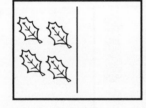

$$\_\_ + \_\_ = \_\_$$

4.

$$\_\_ + \_\_ = \_\_$$

5.

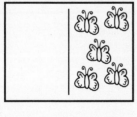

$$\_\_ + \_\_ = \_\_$$

6.

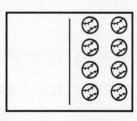

$$\_\_ + \_\_ = \_\_$$

Zero in Addition

Write an addition sentence.

1.

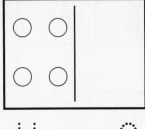

$4 + 0 = 4$

2.

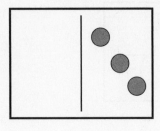

___ + ___ = ___

3.

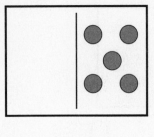

___ + ___ = ___

4.

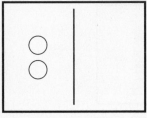

___ + ___ = ___

5.

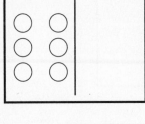

___ + ___ = ___

6.

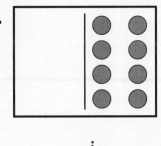

___ + ___ = ___

Problem Solving *Mental Math*

7. You see 2 nests in the tree.

You see 4 baby birds in one nest.

You see none in the other nest.

How many baby birds do you see?

_____ baby birds

Vertical Addition

There are two ways to show addition.

$$
\begin{array}{r}
3 \\
+\ 2 \\
\hline
5
\end{array}
$$

The sum is the same both ways.

$3 + 2 = 5$

Add to find the sum.

1.

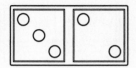

$4 + 3 = \underline{7}$

$$
\begin{array}{r}
4 \\
+\ 3 \\
\hline
7
\end{array}
$$

2.

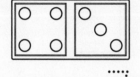

$2 + 5 = \underline{}$

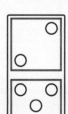

$$
\begin{array}{r}
2 \\
+\ 5 \\
\hline
\square
\end{array}
$$

3.

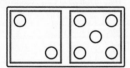

$4 + 2 = \underline{}$

$$
\begin{array}{r}
4 \\
+\ 2 \\
\hline
\square
\end{array}
$$

4.

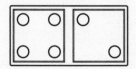

$3 + 5 = \underline{}$

$$
\begin{array}{r}
3 \\
+\ 5 \\
\hline
\square
\end{array}
$$

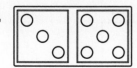

Vertical Addition

Add to find the sum.

1.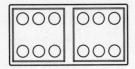

$6 + 6 = \underline{12}$

$$\begin{array}{r} 6 \\ + 6 \\ \hline 12 \end{array}$$

2.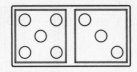

$5 + 3 = \underline{\hspace{1cm}}$

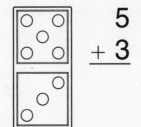

$$\begin{array}{r} 5 \\ + 3 \\ \hline \end{array}$$

3.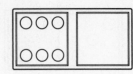

$6 + 0 = \underline{\hspace{1cm}}$

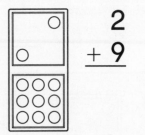

$$\begin{array}{r} 6 \\ + 0 \\ \hline \end{array}$$

4.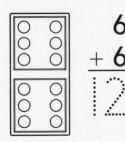

$1 + 9 = \underline{\hspace{1cm}}$

$$\begin{array}{r} 1 \\ + 9 \\ \hline \end{array}$$

5.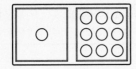

$5 + 6 = \underline{\hspace{1cm}}$

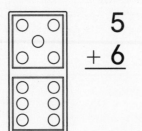

$$\begin{array}{r} 5 \\ + 6 \\ \hline \end{array}$$

6.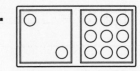

$2 + 9 = \underline{\hspace{1cm}}$

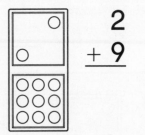

$$\begin{array}{r} 2 \\ + 9 \\ \hline \end{array}$$

Problem Solving *Number Sense*

7. Complete the pattern.

$$\begin{array}{r} 2 \\ + 2 \\ \hline 4 \end{array} \qquad \begin{array}{r} 3 \\ + 2 \\ \hline 5 \end{array} \qquad \begin{array}{r} 4 \\ + 2 \\ \hline 6 \end{array} \qquad \begin{array}{r} 5 \\ + 2 \\ \hline \square \end{array} \qquad \begin{array}{r} \square \\ + \square \\ \hline \square \end{array}$$

Write a Number Sentence

Write an addition sentence to solve a problem.

2 dogs are sitting.
3 dogs are standing.
How many dogs are there in all?

Read and Understand

You need to find how many dogs there are in all.

Plan and Solve

You can write an addition sentence.

$$2 + 3 = 5$$

Look Back and Check

Does your answer make sense?

Write an addition sentence to answer the question.

1. You have 4 books.
   You get 1 more book.
   How many books do
   you have in all?

_____ + _____ = _____

---

2. There are 3 frogs.
   4 more frogs come.
   How many frogs are
   there in all?

_____ + _____ = _____

Write A Number Sentence

Write an addition sentence to answer the question.

1. There are 4 rabbits in the garden.
   5 more rabbits come.
   How many rabbits
   are there in all?

$$4 + 5 = 9$$

2. There are 6 squirrels in the tree.
   5 more squirrels are on the ground.
   How many squirrels are there in all?

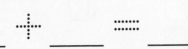
____ + ____ = ____

3. Jane finds 8 shells.
   She finds 4 more shells.
   How many shells does
   Jane have in all?

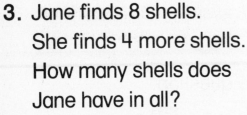
____ + ____ = ____

4. There are 7 apples on the table.
   Tim puts 3 more apples on the table.
   How many apples are on the table?

____ + ____ = ____

Stories About Separating

Count to find how many are left.
Use counters to help you.

Jeff has 5 balloons.
2 balloons fly away.
How many balloons
does he have left?

 balloons

Use counters to answer each question.

1. There are 6 cars.
   2 cars drive away.
   How many cars
   are left?

   [ ] cars

2. There are 7 cats.
   3 are sleeping.
   The rest are playing.
   How many cats
   are playing?

    cats

Stories About Separating

Use counters to answer each question.

1.

There are 5 children at the table.

3 children are eating.

How many children are not eating? ⬜ children

2.

A man has 7 balloons.

2 balloons fly away.

How many balloons does the man have now? ⬜ balloons

Problem Solving *Number Sense*

3. Use counters to answer the question.

There are 6 fish.

2 swim away.

How many fish did not swim away? ⬜ fish

Using Counters to Subtract

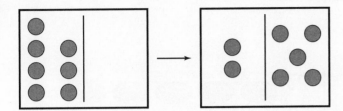

How many counters do we begin with? __7__

How many counters do we take away? __2__

How many are left? __5__

7 take away 2 leaves __5__.

Subtract to find the difference.
Use counters if you like.

1.

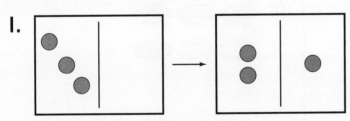

_____ take away _____ leaves _____.

2.

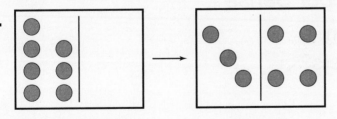

_____ take away _____ leaves _____.

Using Counters to Subtract

Subtract to find the difference.
Use counters if you like.

1.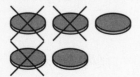

$\underline{4}$ take away $\underline{2}$ is $\underline{2}$.

2. _____ take away _____ is _____ .

3.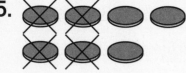

_____ take away _____ is _____ .

4. _____ take away _____ is _____ .

5. _____ take away _____ is _____ .

6.

_____ take away _____ is _____ .

Problem Solving *Number Sense*

7. What is the most you can
take away from 5 counters?
Draw a picture to show
that number.

Using Numbers to Subtract

Subtract to find how many are left.

> This is a subtraction sentence.

_5_	take away	_2_	is	_3_ .
_5_	minus	_2_	equals	_3_ .
5	−	2	=	3

Write a subtraction sentence.

1.

4 minus 1 equals __3__ .

4 — 1 = 3

___ ___ ___

2.

5 minus 2 equals _____ .

___ ___ ___

Problem Solving *Writing in Math*

3. Draw a picture that shows subtraction.
Write a subtraction sentence to go with it.

Name _____

Using Numbers to Subtract

Write a subtraction sentence.

1.  $6 - 2 = 4$	2.  ____ ____ = ____
3.  ____ ____ = ____	4.  ____ ____ = ____
5.  ____ ____ = ____	6.  ____ ____ = ____

Problem Solving *Writing in Math*

7. Draw a picture that shows
   subtraction. Write a
   subtraction sentence to
   go with it.

_____

Zero in Subtraction

If you take away all, zero are left.

$5 - 5 = 0$

$5 - 0 = 5$

If you take away zero, all are left.

Write a subtraction sentence.

1.

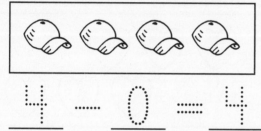

$4 - 0 = 4$

2.

$3 - 3 = 0$

3.

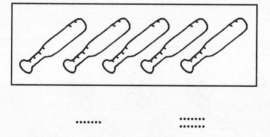

____ .... ____ .... ____

4.

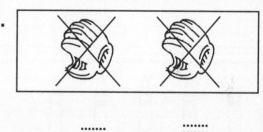

____ .... ____ .... ____

5.

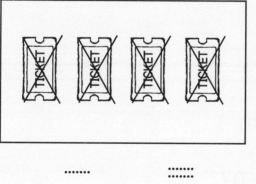

____ .... ____ .... ____

6.

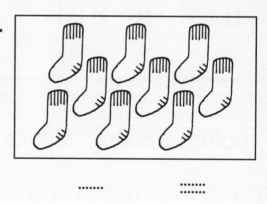

____ .... ____ .... ____

Zero in Subtraction

Write a subtraction sentence.

1.

$$5 - 5 = 0$$

2.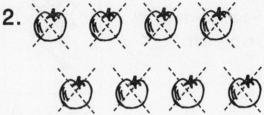

_____ — _____ = _____

3.

_____ .... _____ .... _____

4.

_____ .... _____ .... _____

5.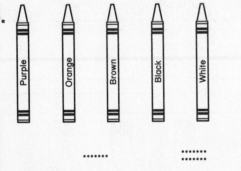

_____ .... _____ .... _____

6.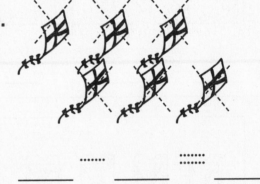

_____ .... _____ .... _____

Problem Solving *Mental Math*

7. If $4 - 0 = 4$, then what is $40 - 0$? _____

8. If $4 - 4 = 0$, then what is $40 - 40$? _____

Vertical Subtraction

There are two ways to show subtraction.

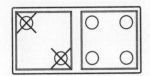

$$6 - 2 = 4$$

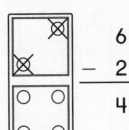

$$\begin{array}{r} 6 \\ -\ 2 \\ \hline 4 \end{array}$$

The answer is the same both ways.

Subtract to find the difference.

1.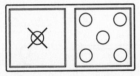

$$8 - 3 = \underline{5}$$

$$\begin{array}{r} 8 \\ -\ 3 \\ \hline 5 \end{array}$$

2.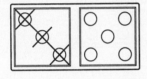

$$6 - 1 = \underline{\hphantom{0}}$$

$$\begin{array}{r} 6 \\ -\ 1 \\ \hline \square \end{array}$$

Problem Solving *Visual Thinking*

Use the dominoes to fill in the missing numbers.

3.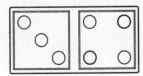

$$7 - \underline{\hphantom{0}} = 4$$

4.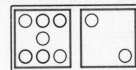

$$\underline{\hphantom{0}} - 7 = 2$$

Vertical Subtraction

Subtract to find the difference.

1.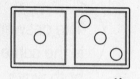

$4 - 1 = \underline{3}$

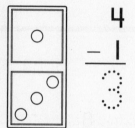

$\begin{array}{r} 4 \\ -\ 1 \\ \hline 3 \end{array}$

2.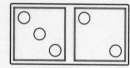

$5 - 3 = \underline{}$

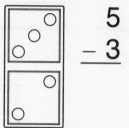

$\begin{array}{r} 5 \\ -\ 3 \\ \hline \end{array}$

3.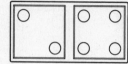

$6 - 2 = \underline{}$

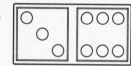

$\begin{array}{r} 6 \\ -\ 2 \\ \hline \end{array}$

4.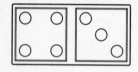

$7 - 4 = \underline{}$

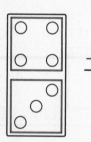

$\begin{array}{r} 7 \\ -\ 4 \\ \hline \end{array}$

5.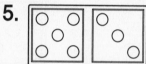

$8 - 5 = \underline{}$

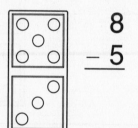

$\begin{array}{r} 8 \\ -\ 5 \\ \hline \end{array}$

6.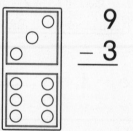

$9 - 3 = \underline{}$

$\begin{array}{r} 9 \\ -\ 3 \\ \hline \end{array}$

Problem Solving *Visual Thinking*

Use the dominos to fill in the missing numbers.

7.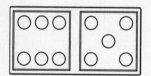

$11 - \boxed{} = 5$

8.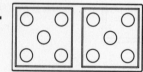

$\boxed{} - 5 = 5$

24 Use with Lesson 2-11.

Name _____

Choose an Operation

Take away 2 flowers.
How many are left?

add   subtract

_____ flowers

Use the picture. Choose **add** or **subtract**.
Write the answer.

1. 6 watermelons are in the garden.
2 are in the basket.
How many watermelons are there in all?

add   subtract

_____ watermelons

---

2. There are 9 carrots.
2 are picked.
How many carrots are left
in the garden?

add   subtract

_____ carrots

---

3. 5 tomato plants are in one row.
6 corn plants are in the same row.
How many plants in all are in the row?

add   subtract

_____ plants

PROBLEM-SOLVING SKILL

Choose an Operation

Use the picture. Choose **add** or **subtract**.
Write the answer.

I. There are 5 ducks in the pond.
   2 ducks fly away.
   How many ducks did not fly away?   add   subtract

   _____ ducks

2. 3 frogs are playing.
   I frog hops away.
   How many frogs did not hop away?   add   subtract

   _____ frogs

3. 2 turtles go for a swim.
   4 more turtles sit on a rock.
   How many turtles are there in all?   add   subtract

   _____ turtles

Using Cubes to Compare

Match the white cubes with the gray cubes.
Then count how many more.

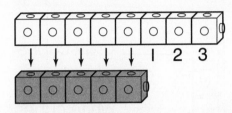

How many more
white cubes?   _3_ more white cubes

How many fewer
gray cubes?   _3_ fewer gray cubes

Write how many white cubes and how many gray cubes.
Then write how many more and how many fewer.

1.
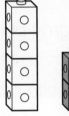

_4_ white cubes

_2_ gray cubes

_2_ more white cubes

2.
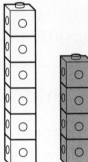

___ white cubes

___ gray cubes

___ more white cubes

3.
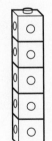

___ white cubes

___ gray cubes

___ fewer gray cubes

4.
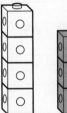

___ white cubes

___ gray cubes

___ fewer gray cube

Using Cubes to Compare

Write how many white cubes and how many gray cubes.
Then write how many more or how many fewer.

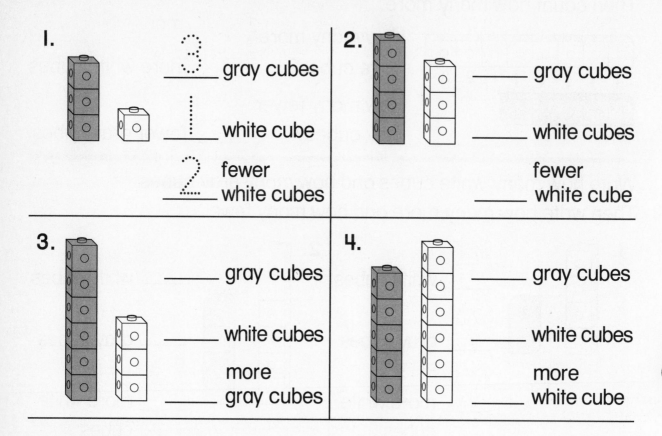

1.

_3_ gray cubes

_1_ white cube

_2_ fewer
___ white cubes

2.

_____ gray cubes

_____ white cubes

fewer
_____ white cube

3.

_____ gray cubes

_____ white cubes

more
_____ gray cubes

4.

_____ gray cubes

_____ white cubes

more
_____ white cube

Problem Solving *Visual Thinking*

5. Draw a picture to solve.
   Dan has 5 model cars.
   Tom has 3 model cars.
   How many fewer model
   cars does Tom have
   than Dan?

   _____ fewer model cars

Using Subtraction to Compare

Write a subtraction sentence to compare.

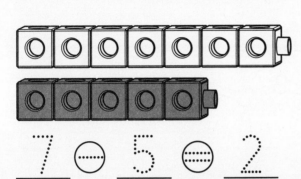

7 ⊖ 5 ⊖ 2

There are __2__ more white cubes than gray cubes.

There are __2__ fewer gray cubes than white cubes.

Write a subtraction sentence.

1. How many more socks than shoes?

_____ ◯ _____ ◯ _____   _____ more socks

2. How many fewer hands than mittens?

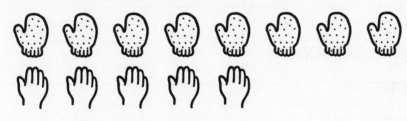

_____ ◯ _____ ◯ _____   _____ fewer hands

Using Subtraction to Compare

Write a subtraction sentence.

Then write how many more or how many fewer.

1. How many fewer dogs than bones?

5 ⊖ 3 ⊜ 2 _____ 2 fewer dogs

_____ _____ _____

2. How many more shoes than socks?

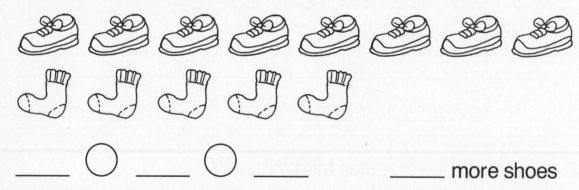

_____ ◯ _____ ◯ _____ _____ more shoes

Problem Solving *Estimation*

Answer each question.

3. Does your class have more boys or more girls?

more _____

4. Does your classroom have fewer children or desks?

fewer _____

Name _____

Bugs, Bugs, Everywhere!

There are 4 ants.
2 more ants join them.
How many ants are
there in all?

Add to find
how many in all.

$4 + 2 = 6$

There are 6 ants.
4 ants leave.
How many ants
are left?

Subtract to find
how many are left.

$6 - 4 = 2$

Circle the correct number sentence.
Write the answer.

1. There are 5 bees on a flower.
   3 bees fly away.
   How many bees are left?

   $5 + 3 = 8$ $5 - 3 = 2$ There are _____ bees left.

2. 7 bugs sit on a leaf.
   2 bugs join them.
   How many bugs are there in all?

   $7 + 2 = 9$ $7 - 2 = 5$ There are _____ bugs in all.

PROBLEM-SOLVING APPLICATIONS

Bugs, Bugs, Everywhere!

1. 4 crickets are chirping.
3 more crickets begin chirping.
How many crickets are chirping now?

4 and 3 more is _____.

2. There are 9 flowers.
There are 7 bees.
How many fewer bees are there?

_____ fewer than 9

3. There are 7 leaves on the flower.
A grasshopper eats 0 leaves.
How many leaves are left on the flower?

_____ − _____ = _____

Writing in Math

4. Write an addition sentence or a subtraction sentence.

_____ ◯ _____ ◯ _____

Write a story about
your number sentence.
Then draw a picture.

Counting On 1, 2, or 3

There are
5 cubes
in the box.

Add
2 more
cubes.

Start
with 5.

Count on
2 more.

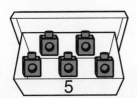

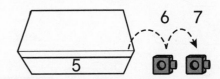

$$5 \quad + \quad 2 \quad = \quad \underline{7}$$

1.

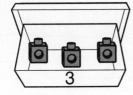

Start with _3_. Count on _1_ more.

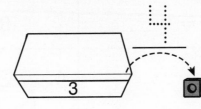

$$3 + 1 = \underline{4}$$

Count on to find the sum.
Use cubes if you like.

2.

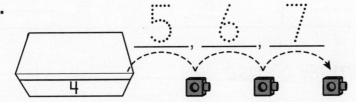

$$4 + 3 = \underline{}$$

3.

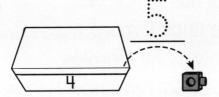

$$4 + 1 = \underline{}$$

Counting On 1, 2, or 3

Count on to solve. Use counters if you like.

1.

5 + 2 = __7__

2.

7 + 1 = _____

3.

6 + 3 = _____

4.

8 + 2 = _____

5.

9 + 3 = _____

6.

6 + 1 = _____

Problem Solving *Number Sense*

Count on to solve.

7. Pam picks 5 flowers.
Then she picks 3 more.
How many flowers does
Pam have in all?

_____ flowers

8. Sal has 7 marbles.
He finds 2 more.
How many marbles
does Sal have now?

_____ marbles

Adding in Any Order

You can add in any order and get the same sum.

$$4 \quad + \quad 2 \quad = 6$$

$$2 \quad + \quad 4 \quad = 6$$

Add. Write an addition sentence with
the addends in a different order.

1.

$$\underline{5} + \underline{2} = \underline{7}$$

$$\underline{2} + \underline{5} = \underline{7}$$

2.

$$\underline{4} + \underline{1} = \underline{}$$

$$\underline{} + \underline{} = \underline{}$$

3.

$$\underline{} + \underline{} = \underline{}$$

$$\underline{} + \underline{} = \underline{}$$

4.
$$\begin{array}{r} 5 \\ + 4 \\ \hline \end{array}$$

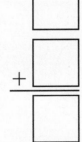

+

5.
$$\begin{array}{r} 3 \\ + 4 \\ \hline \end{array}$$

+

Name _____

Adding in Any Order

Add. Then write an addition sentence with the
addends in a different order.

1.

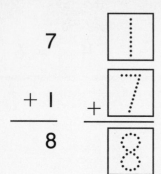

7
+ 1
———
8

+ [ ] [7] [8]

9
+ 2
———
[ ]

+ [ ] [ ] [ ]

6
+ 0
———
[ ]

+ [ ] [ ] [ ]

2.

4
+ 3
———
[ ]

+ [ ] [ ]

6
+ 4
———
[ ]

+ [ ] [ ]

5
+ 2
———
[ ]

+ [ ] [ ]

3. 8 + 3 = _____

___ + ___ = ___

5 + 4 = _____

___ + ___ = ___

6 + 3 = _____

___ + ___ = ___

Problem Solving *Visual Thinking*

4. Write two addition sentences
that tell about the picture.

_____ + _____ = _____

_____ + _____ = _____

8
marbles

Adding 1, 2, or 3

You start with the greater number when you count on.

5   +   2   = _____

5 is the greater number. Count on.

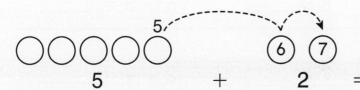

5   +   2   = 7

Circle the greater number. Then count on to add.

1.

(5)   +   1   =

2.

2   +   (6)   =   _____

3.

5   +   3   =   _____

4.

3   +   4   =   _____

5. 5 + 6 = _____	**6.** 7 + 4 = _____	**7.** 1 + 10 = _____
8. 9 + 3 = _____	**9.** 2 + 8 = _____	**10.** 7 + 1 = _____

Name _____

Adding 1, 2, or 3

Circle the greater number.
Then count on to add.

1. (7) + 2 = __9__   1 + 5 = _____   4 + 3 = _____

2. 10 + 2 = _____   3 + 8 = _____   6 + 3 = _____

3. 2 + 8 = _____   1 + 7 = _____   2 + 9 = _____

4.
$$
\begin{array}{cccccc}
2 & 5 & 8 & 11 & 3 & 10 \\
+3 & +2 & +3 & +1 & +7 & +1
\end{array}
$$

5.
$$
\begin{array}{cccccc}
3 & 9 & 2 & 3 & 6 & 3 \\
+1 & +1 & +4 & +8 & +2 & +9
\end{array}
$$

Problem Solving *Algebra*

Finish the picture and complete
the addition sentence.

6.    7.

5 + _____ = 6   3 + _____ = 5

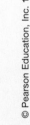

© Pearson Education, Inc. 1

Adding Using a Number Line

To help you count on, circle the number you start at.
Draw to show the addition on the number line.

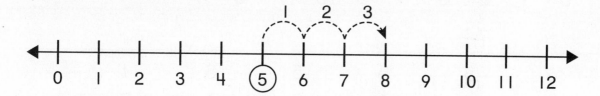

$$5 + 3 = \underline{8}$$

Add 1, 2, or 3. Use the number line to help you.

1. $4 + 3 = \underline{7}$

2. $2 + 6 = \underline{\quad}$

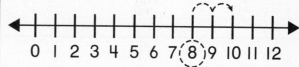

3. $3 + 6 = \underline{\quad}$

4. $8 + 2 = \underline{\quad}$

5.
$$\begin{array}{r} 9 \\ + 3 \\ \hline \end{array}$$

6.
$$\begin{array}{r} 7 \\ + 4 \\ \hline \end{array}$$

Adding Using a Number Line

Add 1, 2, or 3. Use the number line to help you.

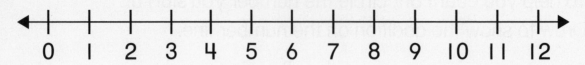

1.	7	6	4	5	8	1
	+ 2	+ 1	+ 2	+ 2	+ 1	+ 7
	9					

2.	3	9	1	6	5	2
	+ 1	+ 2	+ 4	+ 2	+ 3	+ 8

3.	2	7	3	8	9	1
	+ 10	+ 3	+ 6	+ 3	+ 3	+ 11

Problem Solving *Writing in Math*

4. Draw to show the addition on the number line.
Then write the sum.

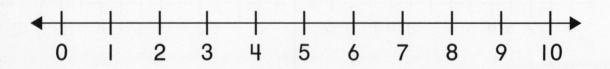

$2 + 6 = $ _____

Name _____

Extra Information

Cross out the information you do not need.
Solve the problem.

> You can underline the sentence that tells what you need to find out.

Dan has 2 dogs.
~~He has one bike.~~
He has 3 cats.
How many pets does Dan have in all?

2 + 3 = 5 pets

Cross out the information you do not need.
Then write a number sentence to solve the problem.

1. Lin read 3 books last month.
   She read 4 books this month.
   2 of the books were about horses.
   How many books did Lin read in all?

   3 + 4 = 7 books

---

2. Tom has 6 model cars. He has 1 model train.
   Tom gets 2 more model cars.
   How many model cars does Tom have altogether?

   _____ + _____ = _____ model cars

---

3. 1 frog jumps in the water. 2 ducks fly away.
   Then 4 more ducks fly away.
   How many ducks fly away in all?

   _____ + _____ = _____ ducks

Extra Information

Cross out the extra information you do not need.

Then write a number sentence to solve the problem.

1. ~~Jane has 8 brown hamsters.~~
   She has 4 black dogs.
   She has 2 tan dogs.
   How many dogs does Jane have?

   __4__ + __2__ = __6__ dogs

2. Dan gets 2 books.
   He reads 8 pages.
   The next day Dan gets
   2 more books.
   How many books did Dan get?

   _____ + _____ = _____ books

3. 4 frogs are on a lily pad.
   Billy wants a pet frog.
   6 frogs are on a rock.
   How many frogs are there?

   _____ + _____ = _____ frogs

4. 5 girls are playing jump rope.
   3 more girls are watching.
   2 boys are playing baseball.
   How many girls are there?

   _____ + _____ = _____ girls

Doubles

● You can use a double to add.

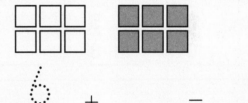

Both addends are the same. They are doubles.

2 + 2 = 4   3 + 3 = 6

Write an addition sentence for each double.

1.

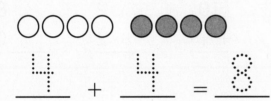

4 + 4 = 8

2.

6 + ___ = ___

3.

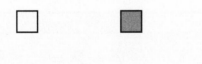

___ + ___ = ___

4.

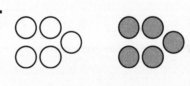

___ + ___ = ___

5.

How many coins are there in all?

___ + ___ = ___

6.

How many coins are there in all?

___ + ___ = ___

Doubles

Circle the doubles. Then add.

1.
$$\begin{array}{r} 7 \\ +\ 1 \\ \hline \end{array}$$
$$\begin{array}{r} 4 \\ +\ 4 \\ \hline 8 \end{array}$$
$$\begin{array}{r} 2 \\ +\ 5 \\ \hline \end{array}$$
$$\begin{array}{r} 6 \\ +\ 6 \\ \hline \end{array}$$
$$\begin{array}{r} 1 \\ +\ 1 \\ \hline \end{array}$$
$$\begin{array}{r} 3 \\ +\ 4 \\ \hline \end{array}$$

2.
$$\begin{array}{r} 4 \\ +\ 3 \\ \hline \end{array}$$
$$\begin{array}{r} 3 \\ +\ 3 \\ \hline \end{array}$$
$$\begin{array}{r} 7 \\ +\ 3 \\ \hline \end{array}$$
$$\begin{array}{r} 2 \\ +\ 8 \\ \hline \end{array}$$
$$\begin{array}{r} 9 \\ +\ 1 \\ \hline \end{array}$$
$$\begin{array}{r} 5 \\ +\ 5 \\ \hline \end{array}$$

3.
$$\begin{array}{r} 0 \\ +\ 0 \\ \hline \end{array}$$
$$\begin{array}{r} 5 \\ +\ 3 \\ \hline \end{array}$$
$$\begin{array}{r} 6 \\ +\ 2 \\ \hline \end{array}$$
$$\begin{array}{r} 10 \\ +\ 1 \\ \hline \end{array}$$
$$\begin{array}{r} 2 \\ +\ 2 \\ \hline \end{array}$$
$$\begin{array}{r} 8 \\ +\ 0 \\ \hline \end{array}$$

4. $9 + 3 =$ _____ $6 + 6 =$ _____ $3 + 6 =$ _____

5. $5 + 5 =$ _____ $8 + 2 =$ _____ $7 + 2 =$ _____

Problem Solving *Visual Thinking*

Write a number sentence to answer each question.

6.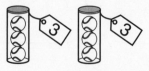

How many balls are there in all?

_____ + _____ = _____

7.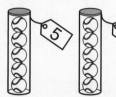

How many balls are there in all?

_____ + _____ = _____

Doubles Plus I

We can use doubles to add other numbers.

2 + 2 and I more

$$2 + 2 = 4$$ $$2 + 3 = 5$$

Find each sum. Use counters if you like.

I.

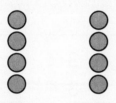

___ + ___ = ___   ___ + ___ = ___

2.

___ + ___ = ___   ___ + ___ = ___

Write a double or a double plus one for each sum.

3.

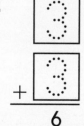   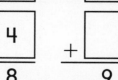

6   7   8   9   10   11

Doubles Plus 1

Find each sum.
Use cubes if you like.

1.
$$\begin{array}{r} 2 \\ +\,2 \\ \hline 4 \end{array} \qquad \begin{array}{r} 3 \\ +\,2 \\ \hline \end{array} \qquad \begin{array}{r} 3 \\ +\,4 \\ \hline \end{array} \qquad \begin{array}{r} 4 \\ +\,4 \\ \hline \end{array} \qquad \begin{array}{r} 6 \\ +\,5 \\ \hline \end{array} \qquad \begin{array}{r} 5 \\ +\,5 \\ \hline \end{array}$$

2.
$$\begin{array}{r} 4 \\ +\,5 \\ \hline \end{array} \qquad \begin{array}{r} 2 \\ +\,3 \\ \hline \end{array} \qquad \begin{array}{r} 0 \\ +\,0 \\ \hline \end{array} \qquad \begin{array}{r} 1 \\ +\,0 \\ \hline \end{array} \qquad \begin{array}{r} 3 \\ +\,2 \\ \hline \end{array} \qquad \begin{array}{r} 1 \\ +\,2 \\ \hline \end{array}$$

3.
$$\begin{array}{r} 1 \\ +\,1 \\ \hline \end{array} \qquad \begin{array}{r} 5 \\ +\,4 \\ \hline \end{array} \qquad \begin{array}{r} 5 \\ +\,6 \\ \hline \end{array} \qquad \begin{array}{r} 6 \\ +\,6 \\ \hline \end{array} \qquad \begin{array}{r} 3 \\ +\,3 \\ \hline \end{array} \qquad \begin{array}{r} 4 \\ +\,3 \\ \hline \end{array}$$

Problem Solving *Algebra*

Write a double or a double plus one for each sum.

4.
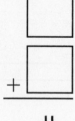   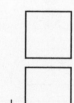

    4   5   6   7   8

Sums of 10

Each ten-frame stands for a group of 10.
You can use a ten-frame to learn sums of 10.

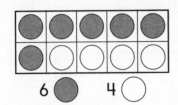

6 + 4 = 10

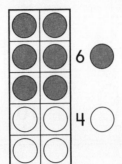

$$6 + 4 \over 10$$

Fill in the missing numbers to find a sum of 10.
Use ten-frames and counters if you like.

1.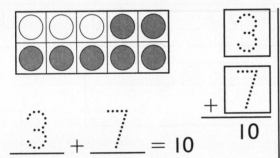

3 + 7 = 10

2.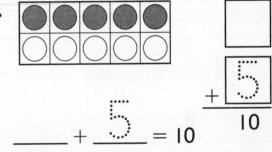

_____ + 5 = 10

3.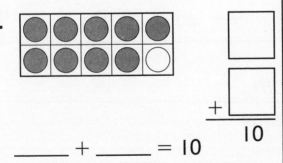

_____ + _____ = 10

4.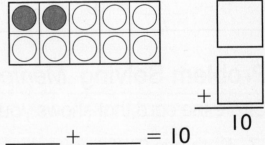

_____ + _____ = 10

---

5. Circle the ten-frame that shows your answer.

Ben has 8 gray counters.
How many white counters does
he need to have 10 counters?

  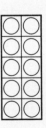

Sums of 10

Fill in the missing numbers to find a sum of 10.
Use ten-frames and counters if you like.

1.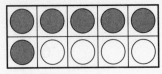

6

+
10

6 + _____ =

2.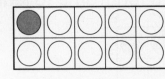

1

+
10

1 + _____ = 10

3.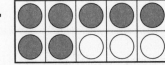

8
+
10

8 + _____ = 10

4.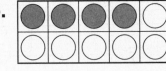

7
+
10

7 + _____ = 10

5.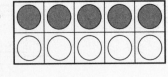

5
+
10

5 + _____ = 10

6.

4

+
10

4 + _____ = 10

Problem Solving *Mental Math*

Circle the card that shows your answer.

7. Beth has 2 stickers.
How many more stickers
does she need to have
10 stickers?

 6   7   8

Name _____

Draw a Picture

There are 4 blue buttons.
There are 3 red buttons.
How many buttons are there?

Blue Buttons	Red Buttons

Read and Understand

You need to find how many buttons there are in all.

Plan and Solve

You can draw a picture of the buttons.
Then you can write a number sentence.
Count the buttons in your picture to find the sum.

$\underline{4} + \underline{3} = \underline{7}$

4 + 3 = 7 buttons

Look Back and Check

How can you be sure your answer is correct?

Draw a picture.
Then write a number sentence.

Bird Stamps   Cat Stamps

1. Dan has 2 bird stamps.
   He gets 4 cat stamps.
   How many stamps are there altogether?

   _____ stamps

   _____ + _____ = _____

Name _____

Draw a Picture

Draw a picture. Then write a number sentence.

1. Dean has 6 stamps.
   He gets 5 more stamps.
   How many stamps does
   he have in all?

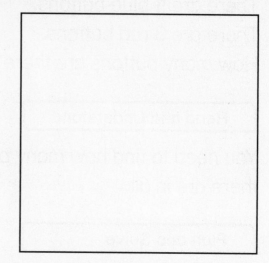

$\underline{6} + \underline{5} = \underline{11}$ stamps

---

2. Jan picks 8 red apples.
   She picks 4 yellow apples.
   How many apples does
   Jan pick in all?

_____ + _____ = _____ apples

---

3. Jo Jo has 4 seashells in her pail.
   She puts 5 more seashells into
   the pail. How many seashells
   are in her pail now?

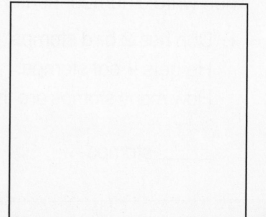

_____ + _____ = _____ seashells

PROBLEM-SOLVING APPLICATIONS

Hop to It!

You can count on to add.

4 rabbits are in the house. 2 more rabbits come.
How many rabbits are there in all?

Start at 4.
Count on 5, 6.
$4 + 2 = 6$.

1.

$5 + 1 = \underline{6}$

2.

$3 + 3 = \underline{}$

3.

$6 + 2 = \underline{}$

4. There are 10 rabbits.
2 of them are in the house.
How many rabbits are outside?

$2 + \underline{} = 10$

5. There are 10 rabbits. 4 of them are outside.
How many rabbits are inside the house?

$4 + \underline{} = 10$

Name _____

Hop to It!

1. 10 rabbits hop into the garden.

   6 of them eat lettuce.

   The rest eat clover.

   How many eat clover?

   $6 +$ _____ $= 10$

2. Kate has 1 cat and 1 bird.

   She has 1 gray rabbit.

   She has 2 white rabbits.

   How many rabbits does Kate have?

   _____ $+$ _____ $=$ _____ rabbits

3. 5 rabbits live in the backyard.

   6 more rabbits come to live with them.

   How many rabbits live in the backyard in all?

   There are _____ rabbits in all.

Writing in Math

4. Draw a picture to show
   8 rabbits in two groups.
   Write an addition sentence for your picture.

Counting Back Using a Number Line

To find 7 − 2,
start at 7. Circle 7.

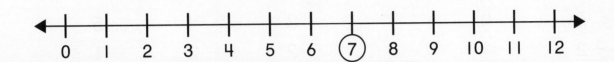

Now count back 2.

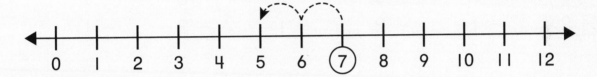

$7 - 2 = \underline{5}$

Count back to subtract.
Show your work on the number line.

I.

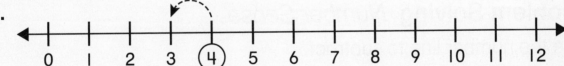

$4 - 1 = \underline{3}$

2.

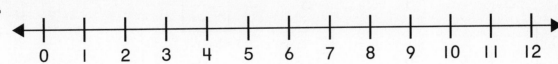

$9 - 2 = \underline{\hphantom{0}}$

© Pearson Education, Inc. 1

Counting Back Using a Number Line

Count back to subtract.

Use a number line if you like.

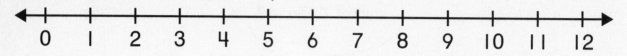

1.

6	4	7	3	4	5
− 2	− 1	− 1	− 2	− 2	− 1

2.

7	6	5	3	8	9
− 2	− 1	− 2	− 1	− 2	− 1

3.

10	9	2	12	12	11
− 1	− 2	− 2	− 1	− 2	− 2

Problem Solving *Number Sense*

Use the number line to subtract.

Write the missing numbers. Look for a pattern.

4.

3	4	5	☐	7	☐
− ☐	− 2	− ☐	− 2	− 2	− 2
1	☐	3	4	☐	6

Counting Back

You can count back to subtract 1 or 2.

5 − 2 = _____

Start at 5.	Count back 2.	Write the number.
	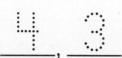 ___, ___	5 − 2 = ___

Count back to subtract.
Use counters if you like.

1.  Count back 2.

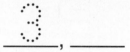 ___, ___   4 − 2 = _____

2.  Count back 1.

___   8 − 1 = _____

3.  Count back 2.

___, ___   10 − 2 = _____

Problem Solving *Number Sense*

4. Kit lost 1 crayon.
   She only has 9 crayons now.
   How many crayons did she start with? _____

Name _____

Counting Back

Count back to subtract.
Use counters if you like.

1.

    $$7$$
    $$-\ 1$$
    $$\overline{6}$$

    Start at 7.
    Count back 1.

2.
$$\begin{array}{r} 11 \\ -\ 2 \\ \hline \end{array}$$
$$\begin{array}{r} 6 \\ -\ 1 \\ \hline \end{array}$$
$$\begin{array}{r} 1 \\ -\ 1 \\ \hline \end{array}$$
$$\begin{array}{r} 7 \\ -\ 1 \\ \hline \end{array}$$
$$\begin{array}{r} 3 \\ -\ 2 \\ \hline \end{array}$$
$$\begin{array}{r} 12 \\ -\ 1 \\ \hline \end{array}$$

3.
$$\begin{array}{r} 5 \\ -\ 1 \\ \hline \end{array}$$
$$\begin{array}{r} 10 \\ -\ 2 \\ \hline \end{array}$$
$$\begin{array}{r} 9 \\ -\ 1 \\ \hline \end{array}$$
$$\begin{array}{r} 3 \\ -\ 1 \\ \hline \end{array}$$
$$\begin{array}{r} 6 \\ -\ 2 \\ \hline \end{array}$$
$$\begin{array}{r} 10 \\ -\ 1 \\ \hline \end{array}$$

4.
$$\begin{array}{r} 2 \\ -\ 1 \\ \hline \end{array}$$
$$\begin{array}{r} 4 \\ -\ 2 \\ \hline \end{array}$$
$$\begin{array}{r} 12 \\ -\ 2 \\ \hline \end{array}$$
$$\begin{array}{r} 8 \\ -\ 2 \\ \hline \end{array}$$
$$\begin{array}{r} 11 \\ -\ 1 \\ \hline \end{array}$$
$$\begin{array}{r} 9 \\ -\ 2 \\ \hline \end{array}$$

Problem Solving *Number Sense*

Use the clues to answer each question.

5. Tao counted back 2.
   His answer was 5.
   On what number
   did he start? _____

6. Adam counted back 1.
   His answer was 11.
   On what number
   did he start? _____

Using Doubles to Subtract

Doubles help you to subtract.

Think: $3 + 3 =$ _6_ so $6 - 3 =$ _3_

Add the doubles.

Then use the doubles to help you subtract.

1.

$1 + 1 =$ _2_ so $2 - 1 =$ _____

2.

$4 + 4 =$ _____ so $8 - 4 =$ _____

Problem Solving *Visual Thinking*

Complete the addition and subtraction sentences.

3. $2 + 2 =$ _____

$4 - 2 =$ _____

Using Doubles to Subtract

Add the doubles.

Then use the doubles to help you subtract.

1.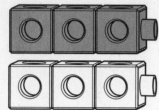

$$\begin{array}{r} 3 \\ +3 \\ \hline 6 \end{array} \qquad \begin{array}{r} 6 \\ -3 \\ \hline 3 \end{array}$$

If $3 + 3 = 6$,
then $6 - 3 = 3$.

2.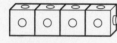

$$\begin{array}{r} 4 \\ +4 \\ \hline \end{array} \qquad \begin{array}{r} 8 \\ -4 \\ \hline \end{array}$$

3.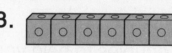

$$\begin{array}{r} 6 \\ +6 \\ \hline \end{array} \qquad \begin{array}{r} 12 \\ -6 \\ \hline \end{array}$$

4.

$$\begin{array}{r} 2 \\ +2 \\ \hline \end{array} \qquad \begin{array}{r} 4 \\ -2 \\ \hline \end{array}$$

5.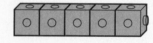

$$\begin{array}{r} 5 \\ +5 \\ \hline \end{array} \qquad \begin{array}{r} 10 \\ -5 \\ \hline \end{array}$$

Problem Solving *Visual Thinking*

Write an addition sentence and a
subtraction sentence for the picture.

6.

_____ + _____ = _____

_____ − _____ = _____

PROBLEM-SOLVING STRATEGY

Write a Number Sentence

There are 6 birds on the branch.
4 birds fly away.
How many birds are left?

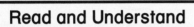

Read and Understand

You need to find how many birds are left.

Plan and Solve

Write a subtraction sentence to find how many birds are left.

$$6 - 4 = 2$$

Look Back and Check

Does your answer make sense?

Write a subtraction sentence to answer each question.

1. There are 8 marbles in the bag.
   3 marbles roll out.
   How many marbles
   are left in the bag?

   _____ _____ _____

---

2. Mary has 10 pencils.
   She gives 4 pencils to Jack.
   How many pencils does
   Mary have left?

   _____ _____ _____

PROBLEM-SOLVING STRATEGY

Write a Number Sentence

Write a subtraction sentence to answer each question.

1. Dana has 6 rings.
   She gives 3 to Lyn.
   How many rings does
   Dana have left?

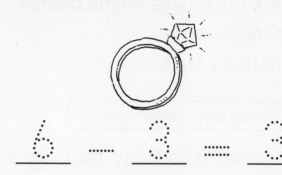

$$6 - 3 = 3$$

2. Ruth has 8 bananas
   and 5 apples on a plate.
   How many more bananas
   does she have?

_____ _____ _____

3. There are 9 cars and
   4 trucks in the parking lot.
   How many more cars
   than trucks are there?

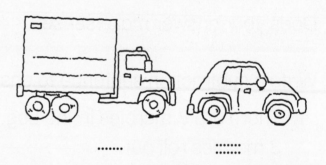

_____ _____ _____

4. 10 birds are eating seeds.
   5 birds fly away.
   How many birds are left?

_____ _____ _____

Using Related Facts

$4 + 3 = 7$

$7 - 3 = 4$

> The addition fact and the subtraction fact use the same numbers.

$6 + 4 = \underline{10}$

$\underline{10} - 4 = \underline{6}$

> The sum of the addition sentence is the first number in the subtraction sentence.

Write a related addition and subtraction sentence for each picture.

1.

$\underline{7} + \underline{4} = \underline{11}$

$\underline{11} - \underline{4} = \underline{7}$

2.

$\underline{} + \underline{2} = \underline{}$

$\underline{} - \underline{2} = \underline{}$

3.

$\underline{} + \underline{} = \underline{}$

$\underline{} - \underline{} = \underline{}$

4.

$\underline{} + \underline{} = \underline{}$

$\underline{} - \underline{} = \underline{}$

Using Related Facts

Write an addition sentence and a subtraction sentence for each picture.

1.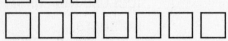

$$\underline{3} + \underline{7} = \underline{10}$$

$$\underline{10} - \underline{3} = \underline{7}$$

> The first number in the subtraction sentence is the sum of the numbers in the addition sentence.

2. △△△△△△△△
△

____ + ____ = ____

____ − ____ = ____

3. ☆☆
☆☆☆☆☆☆

____ + ____ = ____

____ − ____ = ____

4. ♡♡♡♡
♡♡♡♡♡

____ + ____ = ____

____ − ____ = ____

5. ◇◇◇◇◇◇◇◇
◇◇◇

____ + ____ = ____

____ − ____ = ____

Problem Solving *Writing in Math*

Draw a picture to show these related facts.

6. $6 + 3 = 9$ $9 - 3 = 6$

Fact Families

This is a fact family.

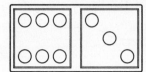

$6 + 3 = 9$ $9 - 3 = 6$

$3 + \underline{6} = 9$ $9 - \underline{6} = 3$

> There are four related facts in this fact family.

This is a fact family, too.

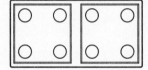

> There are two related facts in this fact family.

$4 + 4 = \underline{8}$ $8 - 4 = \underline{4}$

Write each fact family.

1.

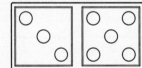

$\underline{3} + \underline{} = \underline{}$ $\underline{} - \underline{3} = \underline{}$

$\underline{} + \underline{3} = \underline{}$ $\underline{} - \underline{} = \underline{3}$

2.

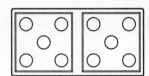

$\underline{} + \underline{} = \underline{}$ $\underline{} - \underline{} = \underline{}$

Fact Families

Complete each fact family.
Use cubes if you like.

> Most fact families have 4 facts.

1.

   $\underline{3} + \underline{4} = \underline{7}$ $\underline{7} - \underline{3} = \underline{4}$

   $\underline{4} + \underline{3} = \underline{7}$ $\underline{7} - \underline{4} = \underline{3}$

2.

   ___ + ___ = ___   ___ − ___ = ___

   ___ + ___ = ___   ___ − ___ = ___

3.

   ___ + ___ = ___   ___ − ___ = ___

   ___ + ___ = ___   ___ − ___ = ___

Problem Solving *Algebra*

Write the missing signs to finish the fact family.

4. 8 ◯ 2 = 10   10 ◯ 8 = 2

   2 ◯ 8 = 10   10 ◯ 2 = 8

Using Addition Facts to Subtract

Use addition facts to help you subtract.

6 − 1 = _____

5 + 1 = 6

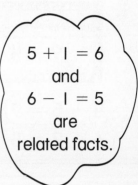

5 + 1 = 6
and
6 − 1 = 5
are
related facts.

6 − 1 = _5_

Match the addition fact that will help you subtract. Then subtract.

1.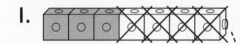

7 − 4 = _3_   5 + 3 = 8

2.

8 − 3 = _____   7 + 2 = 9

3.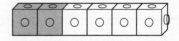

6 − 4 = _____   2 + 4 = 6

4.

10 − 6 = _____   3 + 4 = 7

5.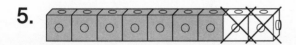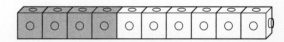

9 − 2 = _____   4 + 6 = 10

Using Addition Facts to Subtract

Circle the addition fact that will help you subtract.
Then subtract.

1. $9 - 4 =$ 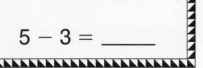 5

$(4 + 5 = 9)$
$6 + 2 = 8$

2. $10 - 6 =$ _____

$8 + 3 = 11$
$4 + 6 = 10$

3. $11 - 8 =$ _____

$5 + 2 = 7$
$8 + 3 = 11$

4. $12 - 4 =$ _____

$4 + 7 = 11$
$4 + 8 = 12$

5. $5 - 3 =$ _____

$3 + 2 = 5$
$5 + 1 = 6$

6. $7 - 4 =$ _____

$4 + 3 = 7$
$5 + 2 = 7$

Problem Solving *Mental Math*

7. May wants to read 9 pages in her book.
She reads 5 pages.
How many pages does
she have left to read?

_____ pages

Choose an Operation

Add to find how many in all.
Subtract to find how many are left.

Marco has 4 pennies.	Maria has 5 pennies.
He gets 2 more pennies.	She gives 3 pennies to Jim.
How many pennies does	How many pennies does
he have in all?	Maria have left?

(add)   subtract

   $4 \oplus 2 = 6$

add   (subtract)

$5 \ominus 3 = 2$

Circle add or subtract.
Then write a number sentence.

1. Ruth has 3 coins.

   She gives 1 coin to Bess.

   How many coins does Ruth have left?

   add   subtract

 ____ ◯ ____ = ____

2. Ned has 4 coins.

   He gets 3 more coins.

   How many coins does he have in all?

   add   subtract

 _____ ◯ _____ = ____

Name _____

Choose an Operation

Circle **add** or **subtract**.

Then write a number sentence.

1. Tom made 6 bookmarks.
He gave away 4 of them.
How many bookmarks
does Tom have left?

add   subtract

____ ◯ ____ = ____

---

2. There are 8 goldfish
in the bowl. Tanya puts in
1 more goldfish. How many
goldfish are there now?

add   subtract

____ ◯ ____ = ____

---

3. There are 4 red apples and
5 green apples. How many
apples are there in all?

add   subtract

____ ◯ ____ = ____

---

4. There are 7 socks.
Jan loses 3 of them.
How many socks are left?

add   subtract

____ ◯ ____ = ____

Name _____

Playful Puppies

5 puppies play.
3 more puppies play.
How many puppies play in all?

___5__ + __3__ = __8__   __8__ puppies play

Solve. Use related facts to help you.

1. 8 puppies are sleeping and
   3 puppies wake up.
   How many puppies are still sleeping?

   _____ – _____ = _____   _____ puppies are sleeping

2. There are 8 puppies.
   There are 4 toys.
   Each puppy wants a toy.
   How many more toys are needed?

   _____ – _____ = _____   _____ more toys

3. There are 6 puppies.
   4 puppies go outside.
   How many puppies are still inside?

   _____ – _____ = _____   _____ puppies are inside

Name _____

Playful Puppies

1. 8 puppies are playing. 5 puppies are sleeping.
   How many more puppies are playing than sleeping?

   _____ – _____ = _____

   There are _____ more puppies playing.

2. 5 puppies are eating. 3 puppies join them.
   How many puppies are eating now?

   There are _____ puppies eating now.

3. There are 10 puppies in a basket. 5 puppies jump out.
   How many puppies are left?

   _____ – _____ = _____

4. Which doubles fact helped you solve Exercise 3?

   _____ + _____ = _____

Writing in Math

5. Write an addition story about grown-up dogs.
   Use pictures, numbers, or words.

Identifying Solid Figures

These shapes are solid figures.

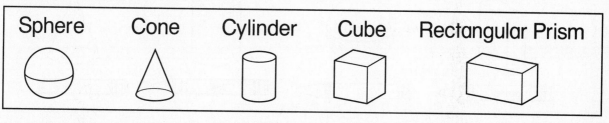

Sphere   Cone   Cylinder   Cube   Rectangular Prism

Color the spheres red. Color the cones blue.
Color the cylinders green. Color the cubes orange.
Color the rectangular prisms yellow.

I.

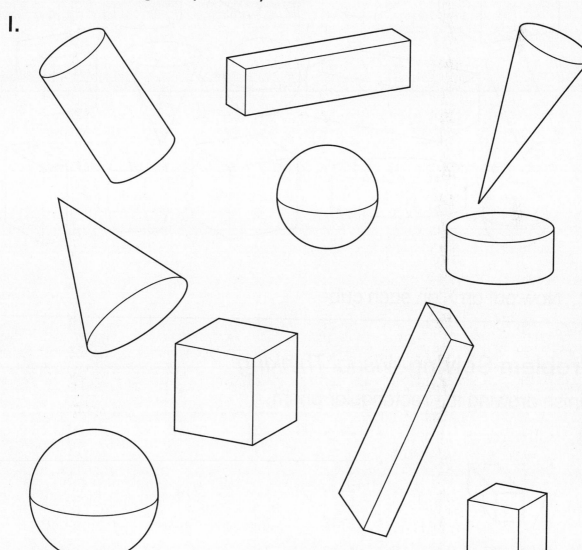

Identifying Solid Figures

1. Color each solid figure below.

green   red   blue   yellow

2. Now put an X on each cube.

Problem Solving *Visual Thinking*

Finish drawing the rectangular prism.

3.

Name _____

Flat Surfaces and Vertices

R 5-2

These solid figures have flat surfaces.

Cone   Cylinder

These solid figures have all flat surfaces called **faces**.

 Rectangular Prism   Cube

These solid figures have **vertices** or corners.

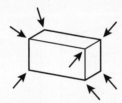 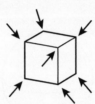

Use solid figures to complete the table.

Solid Figure	Number of Flat Surfaces	Number of Vertices (Corners)	Number of Faces
1. cube	6	8	6
2. cone			
3. rectangular prism			
4. cylinder			

© Pearson Education, Inc. 1

Use with Lesson 5-2. **49**

Flat Surfaces and Vertices

Circle the solid figure that answers each question.

1. Which solid figure has 2 flat surfaces and 0 vertices?

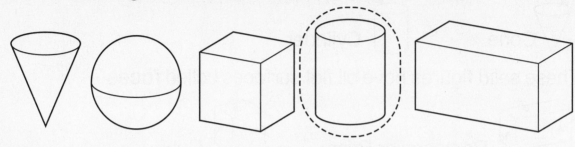

2. Which solid figure has 0 flat surfaces and 0 vertices?

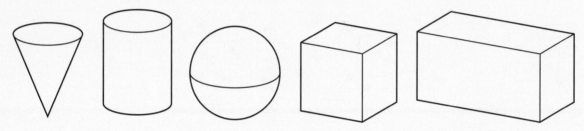

3. Which solid figures have 6 flat surfaces and 8 vertices?

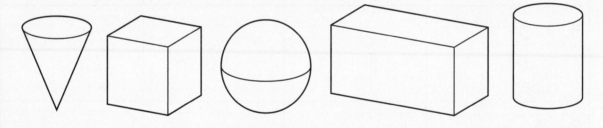

Problem Solving *Reasoning*

Use the clues to answer each question.

4. I have 1 flat surface.
   I have 1 vertex.
   Which solid figure am I?

   _____

5. I have 2 flat surfaces.
   I have no vertices.
   Which solid figure am I?

   _____

Relating Plane Shapes to Solid Figures

If you trace around the flat surface, you can draw a
flat shape. Draw a line to the shape you would make.

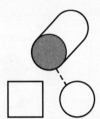 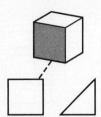 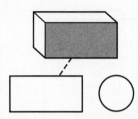

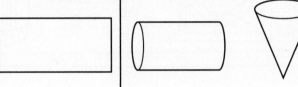 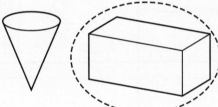

Look at the shape. Then circle the solid figure you
could trace to make the shape.

1.

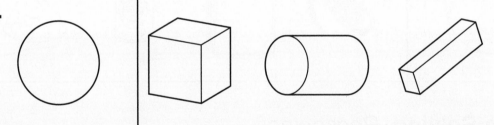

2.

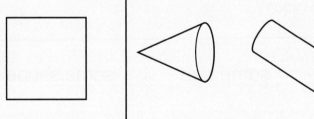

3.

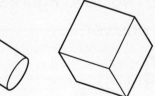

4.

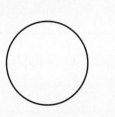 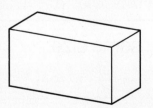  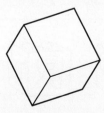

Name _____

Relating Plane Shapes to Solid Figures   **P 5-3**

Look at the shape.
Then circle the objects you could
trace to make the shape.

1.

2.

3.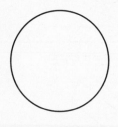

Problem Solving *Reasoning*

How are the two solid figures alike?
Circle each answer.

4.   same size   same shape

5.   same size   same shape

Identifying Plane Shapes

Plane Shapes

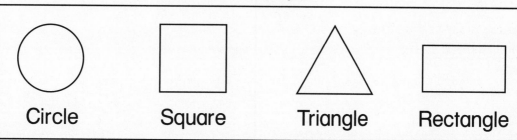

Circle Square Triangle Rectangle

Color the shapes that are the same.
Circle the name.

I.

(square)

triangle

2.

square

circle

3.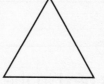

square

triangle

4.

rectangle

triangle

Identifying Plane Shapes

I. Draw a rectangle.

2. Draw a square.

3. Draw a triangle.

4. Draw a circle.

Problem Solving *Algebra*

5. Draw the shape that comes next in the pattern.

Properties of Plane Shapes

Count the straight sides.	Count the vertices.	
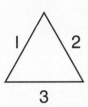	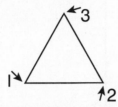	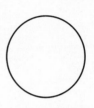
A triangle has 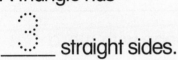 straight sides.	A triangle has 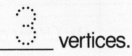 vertices.	A circle has __0__ sides. A circle has __0__ vertices.

I.

A square has _____ straight sides.

A square has _____ vertices.

2.

A rectangle has _____ straight sides.

A rectangle has _____ vertices.

3. Draw a shape with more than 4 vertices.

4. Draw a shape with more than 4 straight lines.

Properties of Plane Shapes

1. Draw a shape with 4 vertices.

2. Draw a shape with fewer than 4 straight sides.

3. Draw a shape with more than 4 straight sides.

4. Draw a shape with more than 4 vertices.

Problem Solving *Reasonableness*

5. Here is the way that Brian sorted some plane shapes.

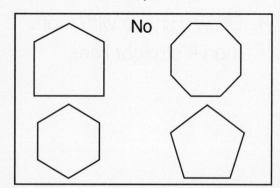

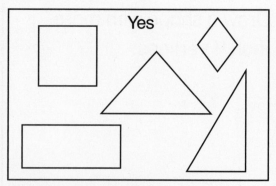

Circle the question that Brian might have asked.

Does it have fewer than 5 vertices?

Does it have more than 5 sides?

Same Size and Same Shape

These rectangles are
the same shape.

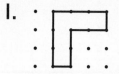

The rectangles are
the same size.
Count the dots to make sure.

These rectangles are
the same shape.

The rectangles are **not**
the same size.
Count the dots to make sure.

Look at the first shape.
Then color the shape that matches it.

I.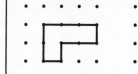

2.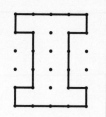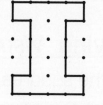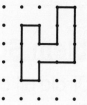

3.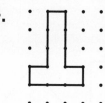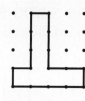

4.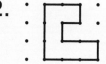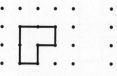

Name _____

Same Size and Same Shape

Look at the first shape.
Then draw two shapes that match it.

1.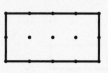

2.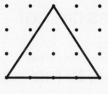

3.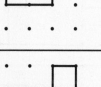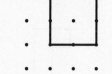

4.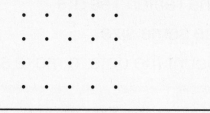

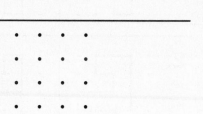

Problem Solving *Visual Thinking*

5. Circle all of the squares.
   Then color the two squares that are
   the same size and the same shape.

 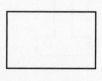

Symmetry

A line of symmetry separates a shape into two matching parts.

These two parts match.

These two parts do not match.

Color the shape that has two matching parts.

1.  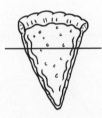	2. 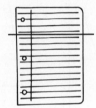 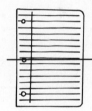
3.  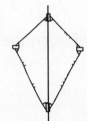	4. 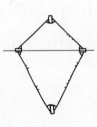

Problem Solving *Visual Thinking*

Draw a different line of symmetry on each circle.

5.

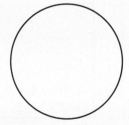  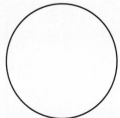 

Symmetry

Draw a **line of symmetry** to make two matching parts.

I. 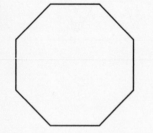	2. 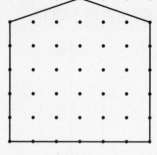	3. 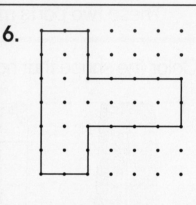
4. 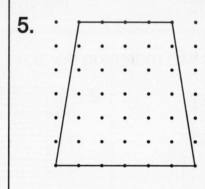	5. 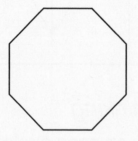	6. 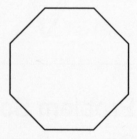

Problem Solving *Visual Thinking*

Draw a different line of symmetry on each shape.

7.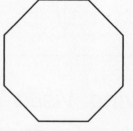

8.

Name _____

Slides, Flips, and Turns

Shapes can slide.	Shapes can flip.	Shapes can turn.
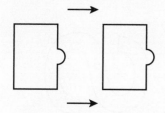	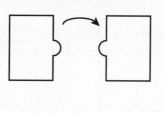	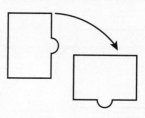

Is it a **slide**, a **flip**, or a **turn**?
Circle the answer.

1.

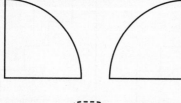

slide   (flip)   turn

2.

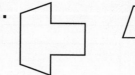

slide   flip   turn

3.

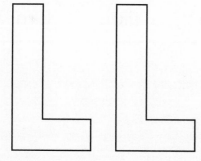

slide   flip   turn

4.

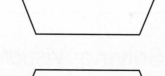

slide   flip   turn

Slides, Flips, and Turns

Is it a **slide**, a **flip**, or a **turn**?
Circle the answer.

1.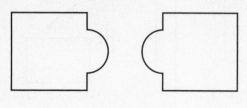

slide   (flip)   turn

2.

slide   flip   turn

3.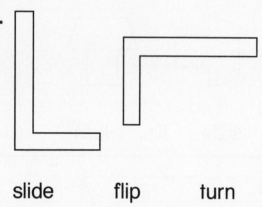

slide   flip   turn

4.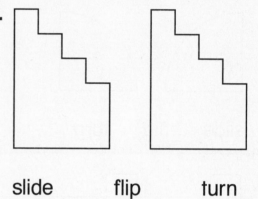

slide   flip   turn

Problem Solving *Visual Thinking*

5. Circle the shapes that will look the same
after they are turned.

           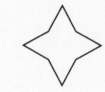

Make an Organized List

Give 3 ways you can make this
shape using pattern blocks.

| Read and Understand |

You need to find all the ways that pattern blocks can make the shape.

| Plan and Solve |

A list can help you keep track.

Ways to Make ⬡			
Shapes I Used	⬠	△	▱
Way 1	1	0	0
Way 2	0	3	0
Way 3	0	1	1

| Look Back and Check |

Did you find 3 ways? How do you know?

Give 3 ways you can make this shape using
pattern blocks. Complete the list.

I.

Ways to Make ▱			
Shapes I Used	⬠	▱	△
Way 1	1	0	1
Way 2			
Way 3			

Name _____

Make an Organized List

1. Show 5 ways you can make
   this shape using pattern blocks.
   Complete the list.

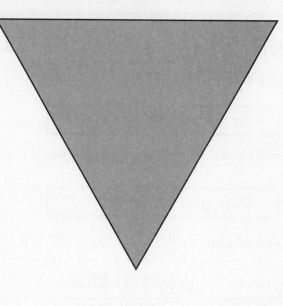

Ways to Make △			
Shapes I Used	⬡	◇	△
Way 1	0	0	9
Way 2			
Way 3			
Way 4			
Way 5			

Writing in Math

2. How many ways can you use
   the pattern blocks to make a ◇ ? Explain.

_____

_____

_____

Equal Parts

This apple pie is divided into equal parts.

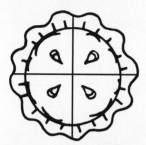

Each part is the same size.

There are __4__ equal parts.

This apple pie is **not** divided into equal parts.

Each part is **not** the same size.

There are __0__ equal parts.

Write the number of equal parts on each shape.

1.

There are __3__ equal parts.

2.

There are _____ equal parts.

3.

There are _____ equal parts.

4.

There are _____ equal parts.

5.

There are _____ equal parts.

6.

There are _____ equal parts.

Equal Parts

Color the shapes that show equal parts.
Then write the number of equal parts
for all of the shapes.

1.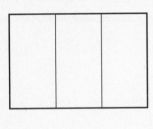

6

2.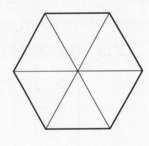

____

3.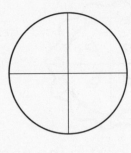

____

4.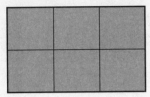

____

5.

____

6.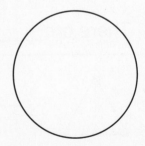

____

Problem Solving *Visual Thinking*

7. Draw straight lines to divide these shapes
into equal parts.

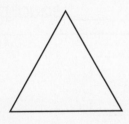

2 equal parts

4 equal parts

4 equal parts

Halves

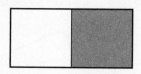

This rectangle has 2 equal parts.
Each part is one half of the rectangle.
$\frac{1}{2}$ is a fraction that means one half.

Circle the shape that shows halves.
Color one half.

1.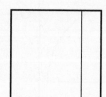

2.

3.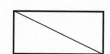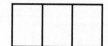

4.

5.

6.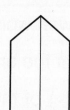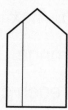

Halves

Draw a straight line on each shape to show halves.

1. 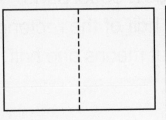	**2.** 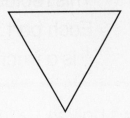	**3.** 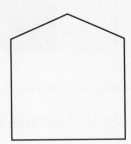
4. 	**5.** 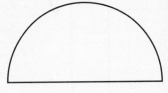	**6.** 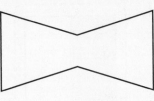
7. 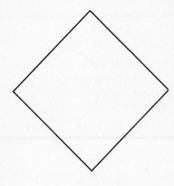	**8.** 	**9.** 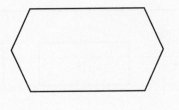

Problem Solving *Mental Math*

10. Ana, Alex, and Gwen want to share

1 orange. They cut the orange in half.

Will each child get $\frac{1}{2}$ of the orange? _____

Thirds and Fourths

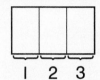

1 2 3

There are 3 **equal** parts. Each part is one third, or $\frac{1}{3}$, of the rectangle.

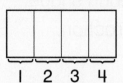

1 2 3 4

There are 4 **equal** parts. Each part is one fourth, or $\frac{1}{4}$, of the rectangle.

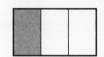

$\frac{1}{3}$ is shaded.

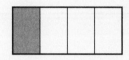

$\frac{1}{4}$ is shaded.

---

1. Circle the shape that shows one third shaded.

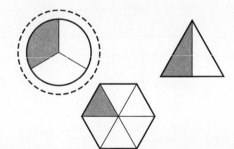

2. Circle the shape that shows one fourth shaded.

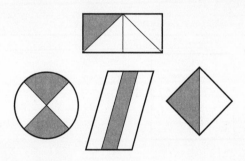

Circle the fraction that shows the shaded part.

3.

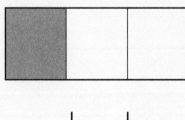

$\frac{1}{3}$ $\frac{1}{4}$

4.

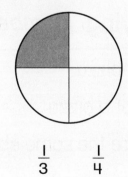

$\frac{1}{3}$ $\frac{1}{4}$

Thirds and Fourths

Color 1 part of each shape.
Then circle the fraction.

1.

$\frac{1}{3}$ $\boxed{\frac{1}{4}}$

2.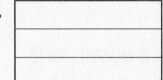

$\frac{1}{3}$ $\frac{1}{4}$

3.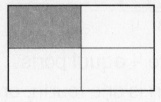

$\frac{1}{3}$ $\frac{1}{4}$

4.

$\frac{1}{3}$ $\frac{1}{4}$

5.

$\frac{1}{3}$ $\frac{1}{4}$

6.

$\frac{1}{3}$ $\frac{1}{4}$

Problem Solving *Number Sense*

7. Jill ate $\frac{1}{3}$ of a pizza.

Mario ate $\frac{1}{4}$ of a pizza.

The pizzas are the same size.

Who ate more pizza?

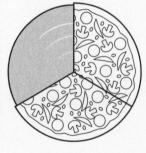 

_____

Name _____

Fractions of a Set

1 ball is gray.	1 ball is gray.	1 ball is gray.
2 balls in all.	3 balls in all.	4 balls in all.
$\frac{1}{2}$ of the balls are gray.	$\frac{1}{3}$ of the balls are gray.	$\frac{1}{4}$ of the balls are gray.

Tell how many are gray. Tell how many in all. Circle the fraction.

1.

_____ hat is gray.

_____ hats in all.

$\frac{1}{2}$ $\frac{1}{3}$ $\left(\frac{1}{4}\right)$

2.

_____ doll is gray.

_____ dolls in all.

$\frac{1}{2}$ $\frac{1}{3}$ $\frac{1}{4}$

3.

_____ yo yo is gray.

_____ yo yos in all.

$\frac{1}{2}$ $\frac{1}{3}$ $\frac{1}{4}$

Circle the fraction that tells what part of the group is gray.

4.

$\frac{1}{2}$ $\frac{1}{3}$ $\frac{1}{4}$

5.

$\frac{1}{2}$ $\frac{1}{3}$ $\frac{1}{4}$

6.

$\frac{1}{2}$ $\frac{1}{3}$ $\frac{1}{4}$

7.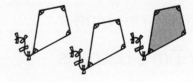

$\frac{1}{2}$ $\frac{1}{3}$ $\frac{1}{4}$

Name _____

Fractions of a Set

Color one object.
Then circle the fraction that tells what
part of the group you colored.

1.

$\frac{1}{2}$ $\frac{1}{3}$ $\frac{1}{4}$

2.

$\frac{1}{2}$ $\frac{1}{3}$ $\frac{1}{4}$

3.

$\frac{1}{2}$ $\frac{1}{3}$ $\frac{1}{4}$

4.

$\frac{1}{2}$ $\frac{1}{3}$ $\frac{1}{4}$

5.

$\frac{1}{2}$ $\frac{1}{3}$ $\frac{1}{4}$

6.

$\frac{1}{2}$ $\frac{1}{3}$ $\frac{1}{4}$

Problem Solving *Writing in Math*

7. Tim has a group of balloons.

   $\frac{1}{3}$ of them are blue.

   Draw Tim's balloons.

Non-Unit Fractions

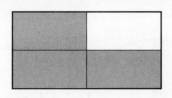

3 parts gray. 4 parts in all.
3 of 4 parts are gray.
$\frac{3}{4}$ of the shape is gray.

3 shapes gray. 4 shapes in all.
3 of 4 shapes are gray.
$\frac{3}{4}$ of the shapes are gray.

Tell how many are gray. Write the fraction.

1.

 of  cars are gray.

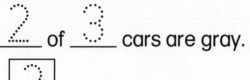 of the cars are gray.

2.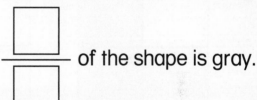

_____ of _____ parts are gray.

$\frac{\quad}{\quad}$ of the shape is gray.

Write the fraction that names the gray part.

3.

4.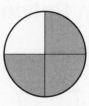

5.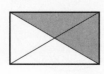

6.

Non-Unit Fractions

Write the fraction that names the shaded part.

1.

2.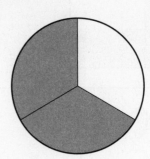

3.

4.

5.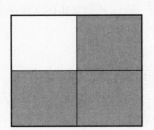

6.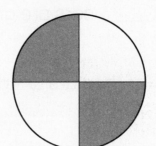

Problem Solving *Number Sense*

7. Color to show $\frac{5}{8}$ on both.

 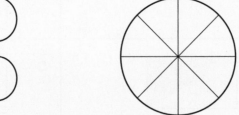

Use Data from a Chart

How can you give an equal share
of plums to each of 6 children?

The chart shows that there are 6 plums.

Use 6 counters.

Fruit		
apples		12
bananas		8
oranges		9
plums		⑥

	José	Juan	Sol
First give one counter to each child.	◯	◯	◯
Then give one more to each child.	◯	◯	◯

Each child gets __2__ plums.

Use the chart and counters to solve.
Draw equal shares.

1.

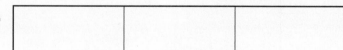

4 children want bananas.

Each child gets __2__ bananas.

2.

3 children want oranges.

Each child gets _____ oranges.

Name _____

Use Data from a Chart

Use the chart and counters to solve.
Draw the equal shares.

Breakfast	
Eggs	12
Muffins	9
Pancakes	8

I. 4 children want to share the pancakes.

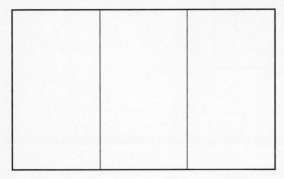

Each child gets __2__ pancakes.

---

2. 3 children want to share the muffins.

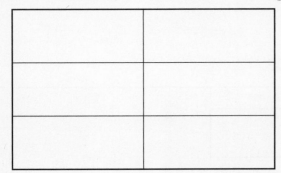

Each child gets _____ muffins.

---

3. 6 children want to share the eggs.

Each child gets _____ eggs.

Shapes All Around Us

  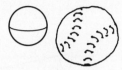 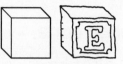 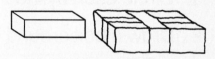

Cone   Sphere   Cube   Rectangular Prism

Find the solids in the picture.
Color the cones red. Color the spheres blue.
Color the cubes green. Color the rectangular prisms yellow.

1. How many cubes did you find? _____ 6

2. How many spheres did you find? _____

3. How many cones did you find? _____

4. How many rectangular prisms did you find? _____

5. Write a number sentence to tell how many
   more cubes there are than spheres.

   _____ – _____ = _____ more cube

Name _____

Shapes All Around Us

1. Circle each cylinder.

2. Draw a box around each cone.

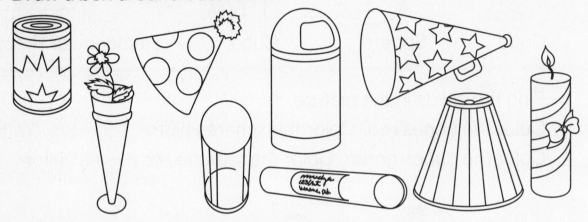

3. How many cylinders did you find? _____ cylinders

4. How many cones did you find? _____ cones

5. Write a number sentence to tell how many more
   cylinders there are than cones.

   _____ – _____ = _____ more cylinder.

Writing in Math

6. Count the cubes and spheres in your classroom.
   Draw a picture of each one of them that you find.
   Did you find more cubes or spheres? How many more?

Minutes

These activities take
less than one minute.

These activities take
more than one minute.

Does the activity take more or less than a minute?
Circle **more** or **less**.

1.

more   (less)

2.

more   less

3.

more   less

4.

more   less

Name _____

Minutes

How long does each activity take?
Circle the correct answer.

1.

Less than 1 minute

(More than 1 minute)

2.

Less than 1 minute

More than 1 minute

3.

Less than 1 minute

More than 1 minute

4.

Less than 1 minute

More than 1 minute

Problem Solving *Estimation*

5. Draw a picture to show
   something that you can
   do in about the same time
   it takes to make your bed.

Understanding the Hour and Minute Hands

The hour hand points to the 6.

hour hand __6__

The minute hand points to the 12.

minute hand __12__

When the minute hand points to 12, say o'clock.

__6__ o'clock

Write the time shown on each clock.

1.

hour hand __3__

minute hand __12__

__3__ o'clock

2.

hour hand _____

minute hand _____

_____ o'clock

3.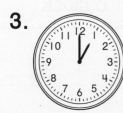

hour hand _____

minute hand _____

_____ o'clock

4.

hour hand _____

minute hand _____

_____ o'clock

Problem Solving *Mental Math*

Write the times that come next.

5. 4 o'clock   5 o'clock   _____ o'clock

6. 9 o'clock   10 o'clock   _____ o'clock

Understanding the Hour and Minute Hands

Draw an hour hand and a minute hand to show each time.

1.  7 o'clock	**2.**  10 o'clock	**3.**  2 o'clock
4.  1 o'clock	**5.**  8 o'clock	**6.**  11 o'clock

Problem Solving *Algebra*

Write the next two hours.

7. 4 o'clock   _____ o'clock   _____ o'clock

8. 8 o'clock   _____ o'clock   _____ o'clock

9. 1 o'clock   _____ o'clock   _____ o'clock

Telling and Writing Time to the Hour

Both clocks show 4 o'clock.

4 tells the hour and...

...00 tells the minutes

4:00

The clocks show the same time.

Draw lines to match the clocks that show the same time.

1.

5:00   7:00

2.

1:00   3:00

3.

12:00   9:00

4.

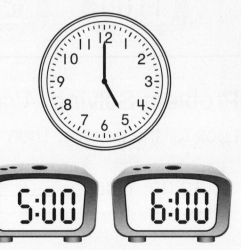

5:00   6:00

Telling and Writing Time to the Hour

Draw lines to match the clocks that
show the same time.

1.

2.

Problem Solving *Algebra*

Look for the pattern. Then write each missing time.

3. 12:00, 1:00, _____ : _____, 3:00, 4:00

4. 10:00, 11:00, _____ : _____, 1:00, 2:00

Telling and Writing Time to the Half Hour

When it is 7:30, the hour hand will be halfway between

__7__ and __8__.

The minute hand

will be on __6__.

The hour hand is shorter than the minute hand.

Complete each sentence.

Then draw the hands on the clock face.

1.

The hour hand will be halfway

between __3__ and __4__.
The minute hand will

be on __6__.

2.

The hour hand will be halfway

between _____ and _____.
The minute hand will

be on _____.

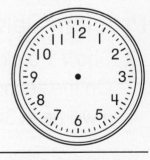

3.

The hour hand will be halfway

between _____ and _____.
The minute hand will

be on _____.

Telling and Writing Time to the Half Hour

Write the time shown on each clock.

1.

2.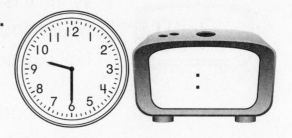

3.

4.

5.

6.

Problem Solving *Visual Thinking*

7. Show 1 o'clock on the first clock.
   On the second clock show the time
   it will be in 30 minutes.

PROBLEM-SOLVING STRATEGY

Act It Out

The game starts at 3:00. It lasts 1 hour. When does it end?

| Read and Understand |

You need to find what time it will be 1 hour after 3 o'clock.

| Plan and Solve |

Show 3 o'clock.   Move the minute hand around the clock one time.   One hour later

 o'clock ——→ 1 hour ——→ o'clock

Write the ending time. Draw the hands on the clock.

1.

 o'clock ——→ 1 hour ——→ _____ o'clock

2.

_____ o'clock ——→ 2 hours ——→ _____ o'clock

Name _____

PROBLEM-SOLVING STRATEGY

Act It Out

P 6-5

Write the starting time and the ending time.
Draw hands on the clock to show the ending time.
Use a clock if you like.

1.

__2__ o'clock ⟶ 2 hours ⟶ __4__ o'clock

2.

_____ o'clock ⟶ 1 hour ⟶ _____ o'clock

3.

_____ o'clock ⟶ 3 hours ⟶ _____ o'clock

© Pearson Education, Inc. 1

68 Use with Lesson 6-5.

Ordering Events

You do things at different times of the day.

morning   afternoon   night

When did each of these things happen?
Write **morning, afternoon,** or **night** on the line.

1.

_____   _____   _____

2.

_____   _____   _____

Ordering Events

P 6-6

When did each of these things happen?
Draw lines to match.

I.

● morning   ● afternoon   ● night

2.

● morning   ● afternoon   ● night

Problem Solving *Writing in Math*

3. Draw a picture to show
   something that you like to do.
   Write **morning, afternoon,** or
   night to match your picture.

Name _____

Estimating Lengths of Time

About how long does each activity take?
You can estimate to find the answer.

 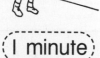  

<u>I minute</u>   I minute   I minute

I hour   <u>I hour</u>   I hour

I day   I day   <u>I day</u>

About how long does each activity take?
Circle your estimate.

I.

Do homework.

    about I minute

    (about I hour)

    about I day

2.

Wash hands.

    about I minute

    about I hour

    about I day

3.

Build a doghouse.

    about I minute

    about I hour

    about I day

4.

Play a game.

    about I minute

    about I hour

    about I day

Estimating Lengths of Time

About how long does each activity take?
Draw lines to match.

I.

about I minute   about I hour   about I day

2.

about 2 minutes   about 2 hours   about 2 days

Problem Solving *Estimation*

3. Jake wants to be a basketball
player. Should he practice
shooting baskets each day
for about I minute or about
I hour?

_____

4. Elaine wants to make a salad.
Will she work for about
5 minutes or about 5 hours?

_____

PROBLEM-SOLVING SKILL   **R 6-8**

Use Data from a Schedule

Nature Center Schedule	
Activity	**Time**
🚶 Hike	9:00
🐢 Feed Turtles	10:00
🌷 Pick Flowers	11:00
🐦 Bird Watch	12:00

A schedule tells the time at which activities start.

Look for the activity.

The hike starts at _9:00_.

Look at the time.

At 12:00 we _bird watch_.

Use the schedule to answer the questions.
Circle your answer.

1. Which activity comes just before feeding the turtles?

    Bird Watch   Hike   Pick Flowers

2. Which activity comes just after picking flowers?

    Hike   Feed Turtles   Bird Watch

3. What time does the activity, Pick Flowers, begin?

    9:00   10:00   11:00

4. Which activity starts at 10:00?

    Hike   Feed Turtles   Bird Watch

Name _____

Use Data from a Schedule

Use the schedule to answer the questions.

Day Camp Schedule	
Time	Activity
9:00	Art
9:30	Tee-ball
10:00	Music
10:30	Puppet Theater
11:00	Swimming

1. What activity do the children do at 9:00? ____Art____

2. What activity do the children do just
   before music? _____

3. What activity do the children do just
   after puppet theater? _____

4. What time does music begin? _____

Problem Solving *Reasonableness*

5. The children are about to start music.
   Ned wants to know how long it is until
   it is time for swimming. Lou says it is
   about 1 hour. Is he correct? _____

Days of the Week

March

	1st day	2nd day	3rd day	4th day	5th day	6th day	7th day
	Sunday	Monday	Tuesday	Wednesday	Thursday	Friday	Saturday
			1	2	3	4	5
	6	7	8	9	10	11	12
	13	14	15	16	17	18	19
	20	21	22	23	24	25	26
	27	28	29	30	31		

There are 7 days in a week.

Use the calendar to answer the questions.

1. Write the days of the week in order.

   Sunday, __Monday__, Tuesday, _____,

   Thursday, _____, _____

2. Color all the Saturdays yellow.   ⬛ yellow ⬛▷

3. Color all the Mondays blue.   ⬛ blue ⬛▷

Problem Solving *Visual Thinking*

4. Find the pattern.
   Then write the day of the week that comes next.

   Wednesday, Thursday, _____, Saturday

5. Monday, Tuesday, _____, Thursday

Days of the Week

1. Circle the names of the days of the week.

2. Color the Mondays blue and Wednesdays red.

April						
Sunday	Monday	Tuesday	Wednesday	Thursday	Friday	Saturday
	1	2	3	4	5	6
7	8	9	10	11	12	13
14	15	16	17	18	19	20
21	22	23	24	25	26	27
28	29	30				

3. Write the days of the week in order.

Sunday _____, Monday _____, _____,

_____, _____, _____,

_____

Problem Solving *Visual Thinking*

Find the pattern. Then write the day that comes next.

4. | Wednesday | | Thursday | | Friday | _____

5. | Friday | | Saturday | | Sunday | _____

Months of the Year

> January is the first month of the year.

> February is the month **before** March.

> **March** is the third month.

> April is the month **after** March.

January						
S	M	T	W	T	F	S
					1	2	3
4	5	6	7	8	9	10
11	12	13	14	15	16	17
18	19	20	21	22	23	24
25	26	27	28	29	30	31

February						
S	M	T	W	T	F	S
1	2	3	4	5	6	7
8	9	10	11	12	13	14
15	16	17	18	19	20	21
22	23	24	25	26	27	28

March						
S	M	T	W	T	F	S
1	2	3	4	5	6	7
8	9	10	11	12	13	14
15	16	17	18	19	20	21
22	23	24	25	26	27	28
29	30	31				

April						
S	M	T	W	T	F	S
				1	2	3	4
5	6	7	8	9	10	11
12	13	14	15	16	17	18
19	20	21	22	23	24	25
26	27	28	29	30		

May						
S	M	T	W	T	F	S
					1	2
3	4	5	6	7	8	9
10	11	12	13	14	15	16
17	18	19	20	21	22	23
24/31	25	26	27	28	29	30

June						
S	M	T	W	T	F	S
	1	2	3	4	5	6
7	8	9	10	11	12	13
14	15	16	17	18	19	20
21	22	23	24	25	26	27
28	29	30				

July						
S	M	T	W	T	F	S
				1	2	3	4
5	6	7	8	9	10	11
12	13	14	15	16	17	18
19	20	21	22	23	24	25
26	27	28	29	30	31	

August						
S	M	T	W	T	F	S
						1
2	3	4	5	6	7	8
9	10	11	12	13	14	15
16	17	18	19	20	21	22
23/30	24/31	25	26	27	28	29

September						
S	M	T	W	T	F	S
		1	2	3	4	5
6	7	8	9	10	11	12
13	14	15	16	17	18	19
20	21	22	23	24	25	26
27	28	29	30			

October						
S	M	T	W	T	F	S
				1	2	3
4	5	6	7	8	9	10
11	12	13	14	15	16	17
18	19	20	21	22	23	24
25	26	27	28	29	30	31

November						
S	M	T	W	T	F	S
1	2	3	4	5	6	7
8	9	10	11	12	13	14
15	16	17	18	19	20	21
22	23	24	25	26	27	28
29	30					

December						
S	M	T	W	T	F	S
		1	2	3	4	5
6	7	8	9	10	11	12
13	14	15	16	17	18	19
20	21	22	23	24	25	26
27	28	29	30	31		

Use the calendar to answer the questions.

1. What are the names of the months?

   January, February, _____March_____, April, May,

   _____, July, August, _____,

   October, November, _____

2. Count the months. How many months are in a year? _____

3. Which month is the first month of the year? _____

4. Which month comes after May? _____

5. Which month comes before September? _____

Months of the Year

January
S M T W T F S
· · · · 1 2 3
4 5 6 7 8 9 10
11 12 13 14 15 16 17
18 19 20 21 22 23 24
25 26 27 28 29 30 31

February
S M T W T F S
1 2 3 4 5 6 7
8 9 10 11 12 13 14
15 16 17 18 19 20 21
22 23 24 25 26 27 28

March
S M T W T F S
1 2 3 4 5 6 7
8 9 10 11 12 13 14
15 16 17 18 19 20 21
22 23 24 25 26 27 28
29 30 31

April
S M T W T F S
· · · 1 2 3 4
5 6 7 8 9 10 11
12 13 14 15 16 17 18
19 20 21 22 23 24 25
26 27 28 29 30

May
S M T W T F S
· · · · · 1 2
3 4 5 6 7 8 9
10 11 12 13 14 15 16
17 18 19 20 21 22 23
24/31 25 26 27 28 29 30

June
S M T W T F S
· 1 2 3 4 5 6
7 8 9 10 11 12 13
14 15 16 17 18 19 20
21 22 23 24 25 26 27
28 29 30

July
S M T W T F S
· · · 1 2 3 4
5 6 7 8 9 10 11
12 13 14 15 16 17 18
19 20 21 22 23 24 25
26 27 28 29 30 31

August
S M T W T F S
· · · · · · 1
2 3 4 5 6 7 8
9 10 11 12 13 14 15
16 17 18 19 20 21 22
23/30 24/31 25 26 27 28 29

September
S M T W T F S
· · 1 2 3 4 5
6 7 8 9 10 11 12
13 14 15 16 17 18 19
20 21 22 23 24 25 26
27 28 29 30

October
S M T W T F S
· · · · 1 2 3
4 5 6 7 8 9 10
11 12 13 14 15 16 17
18 19 20 21 22 23 24
25 26 27 28 29 30 31

November
S M T W T F S
1 2 3 4 5 6 7
8 9 10 11 12 13 14
15 16 17 18 19 20 21
22 23 24 25 26 27 28
29 30

December
S M T W T F S
· · 1 2 3 4 5
6 7 8 9 10 11 12
13 14 15 16 17 18 19
20 21 22 23 24 25 26
27 28 29 30 31

1. Write the names of the missing months.

January, February, _____March_____, _____,

_____, June, July, _____,

_____, October, _____, December

Problem Solving *Number Sense*

You can show the date two ways.

April 19, 2004 or **4/19/04**

2. Draw lines to match the dates.

August 22, 2004   5/9/04

May 9, 2004   8/22/04

> The 4 tells that April is the 4th month.

PROBLEM-SOLVING APPLICATIONS

What's Inside the Egg?

1. Jane uses a telescope to look at the birds.

What shape is the telescope?

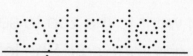

cylinder

2. At 3 o'clock Jane sees a baby bird.
   Write the time on both clocks.

3. On Monday 1 bird egg hatches.
   The next day 2 bird eggs hatch.
   On what day do the 2 bird eggs hatch?   _____

Writing in Math

4. It is April. In 2 months Jane will
   get a pet bird for her birthday.
   In what month is Jane's birthday?   _____

Name _____

What's Inside the Egg?

1. The zoo keeps baby
tortoises in this tank.
What shape is the tank?

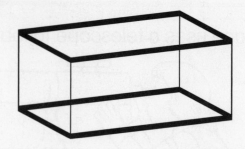

_____

2. Joan went to the zoo to see
the baby tortoises. She left
the zoo at 4:30. Show the
time on both clocks.

3. Joan wanted to go to the
zoo on Monday. Her mother
took Joan the next day. On
which day did Joan go to
the zoo?

_____

Writing in Math

4. Joan visited the zoo in April.
After 3 months, she will go
back to see how much the
baby tortoises have grown.
Use a calendar to find which
month she will return to the zoo.

_____

Numbers to 19

Use counters and Workmat 3.
Write each number as 10 and some left over.

 This shows 10.

 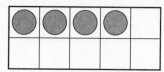

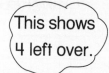 This shows 4 left over.

14 is __10__ and __4__.

1.

 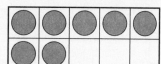

17 is __10__ and __7__.

2.

16 is _____ and __6__.

3.

 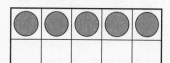

15 is _____ and _____.

4.

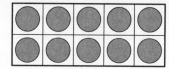 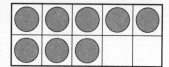

18 is _____ and _____.

Name _____

Numbers to 19

Use Counters and Workmat 3.

Write each number as 10 and some left over.

1. | twelve | 12 is __10__ and __2__.

2. | eighteen | 18 is _____ and _____.

3. | fourteen | 14 is _____ and _____.

4. | eleven | 11 is _____ and _____.

5. | seventeen | 17 is _____ and _____.

6. | nineteen | 19 is _____ and _____.

7. | sixteen | 16 is _____ and _____.

Problem Solving *Algebra*

Write each missing number.

8. ☐ and 10 is 13.

9. 2 and ☐ is 12.

10. 10 and ☐ is 16.

11. ☐ and 8 is 18.

12. ☐ and 10 is 17.

13. 5 and ☐ is 15.

Name _____

Counting by 10s to 100

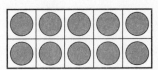 stands for one group of ten.

10,	20,	30,	40,	50,
ten,	twenty,	thirty,	forty,	fifty,
60,	70,	80,	90,	100,
sixty,	seventy,	eighty,	ninety,	one hundred

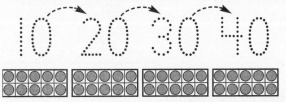

$\underline{4}$ groups of ten

$\underline{40}$ forty

Count by 10s. Then write the numbers.

1.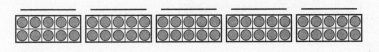

$\underline{5}$ groups of ten

fifty

2.

_____ groups of ten

_____ _____

3.

_____ groups of ten

_____ _____

Name _____

Counting by 10s to 100

10,	20,	30,	40,	50,
ten,	twenty,	thirty,	forty,	fifty,
60,	70,	80,	90,	100
sixty,	seventy,	eighty,	ninety,	one hundred

Count by tens. Then write the numbers.

1. ___4___ groups of 10

___40___

___forty___

2. _____ groups of 10

_____

_____

3. _____ groups of 10

_____

_____

Problem Solving *Mental Math*

4. Laura saves 10¢ each day. How much money has she saved after 5 days?

_____¢

5. Kit saves 10¢ each day. How much money has he saved after 7 days?

_____¢

Hundred Chart

Use the hundred chart.
Count on from 24.

Start at 24.
Count on by 1s.

24, _25_, _26_, _27_

1	2	3	4	5	6	7	8	9	10
11	12	13	14	15	16	17	18	19	20
21	22	23	(24)	25	26	27	28	29	30
31	32	33	34	35	36	37	38	39	40
41	42	43	44	45	46	47	48	49	50
51	52	53	(54)	55	56	57	58	59	60
61	62	63	64	65	66	67	68	69	70
71	72	73	74	75	76	77	78	79	80
81	82	83	84	85	86	87	88	89	90
91	92	93	94	95	96	97	98	99	100

Count back from 54.

Start at 54.
Count back
by 1s.

54, _53_, _52_, _51_

Write the missing numbers. Look for patterns.

1.

41	42				46	47			
51	52		54	55			58	59	
		63			66	67			70
			74	75			78		

Use the hundred chart to count back by 1s.

2. 29, _28_, _27_, 26 ____, ____, 23

3. 31, _30_, ____, ____, 27, ____, ____

Hundred Chart

1. Write the missing numbers. Look for patterns.

1	2								
11	12	13	14	15	16	17	18	19	20
31	32	33	34	35	36	37	38	39	40
							48	49	50
					56	57	58	59	60
61	62	63	64	65					
					76	77	78	79	80
81	82	83	84						90
91					96	97	98	99	100

Use the hundred chart above to count back by ones.

2. 79, _78_, _77_, _____, _____, _____, _____

3. 31, _____, _____, _____, _____, _____, _____

Problem Solving *Number Sense*

Look at these parts of the hundred chart.
Write the missing numbers.

4.

42		
	53	55

5.

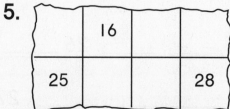

	16	
25		28

Name _____

Counting with Groups of 10 and Leftovers

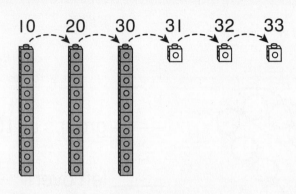

__3__ groups of 10   __3__ left over   __33__ in all

Use counters to show the snap cubes.
Make groups of 10.
Then write the numbers.

1. 10 20 21 22 23 24 25 26 27

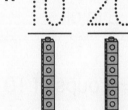

__2__ groups of ten

__7__ left over

_____ in all

2.

_____ groups of ten

_____ left over

_____ in all

Counting with Groups of 10 and Leftovers

Circle groups of 10 beads.
Then write the numbers.

I.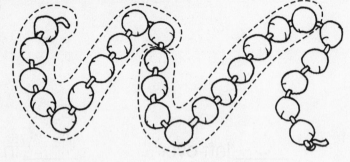

_2_ groups of 10

_5_ left over

_25_ in all

2.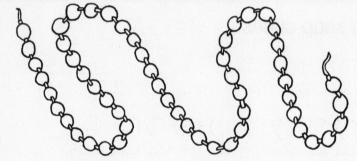

_____ groups of 10

_____ left over

_____ in all

3.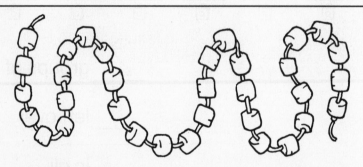

_____ groups of 10

_____ left over

_____ in all

Problem Solving *Visual Thinking*

Draw a picture to solve.

4. Ben has 25 beads. 10 beads fit on a key chain.
How many
key chains can he make? _____

How many beads
will be left over? _____

Estimating with Groups of 10

An estimate tells **about** how many.

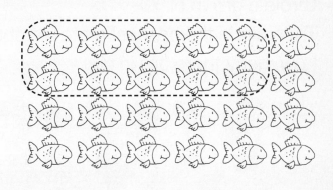

Circle 10 fish.
About how many more groups
of 10 fish do you see?

There are about   10   20   30 fish in all.

Circle a group of 10. Then circle the best estimate
for how many there are in all.

1.

about 10   30   50

2.

about 10   20   30

Name _____

Estimating with Groups of 10

Circle a group of 10.
Then circle the best estimate for about
how many there are in all.

1.

about

20   (50)   70

2.

about

20   40   60

3.

about

10   30   50

Problem Solving *Estimation*

4. Circle all of the numbers that answer the question.

   Tammy estimates that she has about 30 stamps.
   Which numbers could show how many stamps
   Tammy really has?

   21   28   32   39   41   48   52

Use Data from a Graph

This graph shows how many birds are in the park.
How many pigeons are there? Count by 10s.

Birds	
Sparrows	⊞⊞
Pigeons	⊞⊞ ⊞⊞ ⊞⊞
Robins	⊞⊞ ⊞⊞

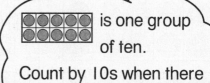

is one group
of ten.
Count by 10s when there
is more than one group.

There are ____3____ groups of 10.

There are ___30___ pigeons.

Use the graph to answer each question.

1. How many sparrows are there?   There is _____ group of 10.

   There are _____ sparrows.

2. Of which kind of bird is
   there the most?   _____

3. How many pigeons and
   robins are there altogether?   _____

4. How many more pigeons than
   sparrows are there?   _____

PROBLEM-SOLVING SKILL

Use Data from a Graph

Our Pets		
Dogs	Cats	Fish

Use the graph to answer each question.

1. Of which pet are there the most? _____

2. Of which pet are there the fewest? _____

3. How many more fish are there than cats? _____

4. How many dogs and cats are there altogether? _____

Writing in Math

5. Write your own question about the graph.

_____

_____

Skip-Counting Patterns on the Hundred Chart

Skip count by 10s on the hundred chart.

1	2	3	4	5	6	7	8	9	10		10
11	12	13	14	15	16	17	18	19	20		20
21	22	23	24	25	26	27	28	29	30		30
31	32	33	34	35	36	37	38	39	40		40
41	42	43	44	45	46	47	48	49	50		50
51	52	53	54	55	56	57	58	59	60		60
61	62	63	64	65	66	67	68	69	70		70
71	72	73	74	75	76	77	78	79	80		80
81	82	83	84	85	86	87	88	89	90		90
91	92	93	94	95	96	97	98	99	100		100

When you skip count by 10s all of the numbers end in 0.

1. Skip count by 5s. Draw a square around the numbers you say.

2. When you skip count by 5s, all of the numbers end in

_____ or _____.

1	2	3	4	5	6	7	8	9	10
11	12	13	14	15	16	17	18	19	20
21	22	23	24	25	26	27	28	29	30
31	32	33	34	35	36	37	38	39	40
41	42	43	44	45	46	47	48	49	50
51	52	53	54	55	56	57	58	59	60
61	62	63	64	65	66	67	68	69	70
71	72	73	74	75	76	77	78	79	80
81	82	83	84	85	86	87	88	89	90
91	92	93	94	95	96	97	98	99	100

Skip-Counting Patterns
on the Hundred Chart

I. Color the numbers you say when you count by fives.

1	2	3	4	5	6	7	8	9	10
11	12	13	14	15	16	17	18	19	20
21	22	23	24	25	26	27	28	29	30
31	32	33	34	35	36	37	38	39	40
41	42	43	44	45	46	47	48	49	50
51	52	53	54	55	56	57	58	59	60
61	62	63	64	65	66	67	68	69	70
71	72	73	74	75	76	77	78	79	80
81	82	83	84	85	86	87	88	89	90
91	92	93	94	95	96	97	98	99	100

2. Color the numbers you say when you count by twos.

61	62	63	64	65	66	67	68	69	70
71	72	73	74	75	76	77	78	79	80
81	82	83	84	85	86	87	88	89	90
91	92	93	94	95	96	97	98	99	100

Problem Solving *Visual Thinking*

Finish coloring the calendar. Write **yes** or **no**.

3. Vicki has baseball practice every 5 days.
   Will she have practice on May 19? _____

May						
Sunday	Monday	Tuesday	Wednesday	Thursday	Friday	Saturday
	1	2	3	4	5	6
7	8	9	10	11	12	13
14	15	16	17	18	19	20

Using Skip Counting

Skip count to find how many.

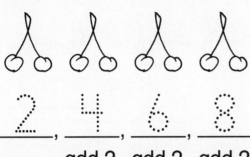

Skip count by 2, or add 2 to the last number.

_2_, _4_, _6_, _8_
　　　add 2　add 2　add 2

_8_
There are ___ cherries.

---

1. Skip count by 2s.

_2_, _4_, ____, ____, ____, ____

---

2. Skip count by 5s.

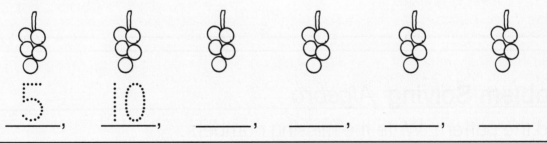

_5_, _10_, ____, ____, ____, ____

---

3. Skip count by 10s.

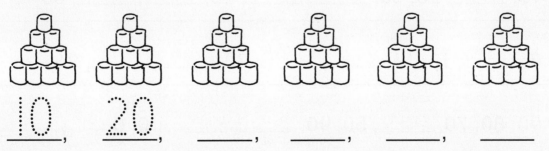

_10_, _20_, ____, ____, ____, ____

Name _____

Using Skip Counting

1. How many ears are there?

Count by twos.

2, _____, _____, _____, _____, _____, _____

2. How many cans are there?

Count by fives.

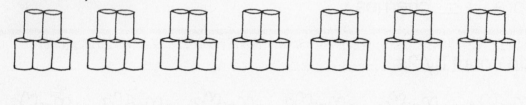

_____, _____, _____, _____, _____, _____, _____

3. How many balls are there?

Count by tens.

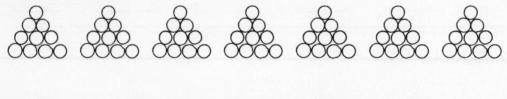

_____, _____, _____, _____, _____, _____, _____

Problem Solving *Algebra*

Find the pattern. Write the missing numbers.

4. 15, _____, 25, 30, _____, _____, 45, _____, _____, 60

5. 8, _____, 12, 14, _____, _____, 20, _____, _____, 26

6. 90, 80, 70, _____, 50, 40, _____, _____, 10, 0

Name _____

PROBLEM-SOLVING STRATEGY

Name _____

PROBLEM-SOLVING STRATEGY   R 7-9

Look for a Pattern

The children need mittens.

Each child has two hands.

How many mittens are needed for all of the children?

Read and Understand

You need to find how many hands the children have altogether.

Plan and Solve

Make a table to show a pattern. Write the numbers.

Count the children by 1s.

Count the mittens by 2s.

Number of Children	1	2		
Number of Mittens	2	4		

8

_____ mittens will be needed for all of the children.

Look Back and Check

Does your answer make sense?

Find the pattern. Write the numbers.

1. There are 4 boxes.
   Each box has 5 crayons.
   How many crayons are
   there in all?

Number of Boxes	1	2		
Number of Crayons	5			

There are _____ crayons in all.

© Pearson Education, Inc. 1

Use with Lesson 7-9. **83**

Name _____

Look for a Pattern

Find a pattern. Then write the numbers.

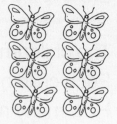

1. There are 6 butterflies. Each butterfly has 4 wings.
How many wings are on the butterflies altogether?

Number of Butterflies	1					
Number of Wings	4					

There are _____ wings in all on the butterflies.

---

2. There are 5 cows. Each cow has 4 legs.
How many legs are on the cows altogether?

Number of Cows					
Number of Legs					

There are _____ legs in all on the cows.

---

3. There are 7 boxes.
Each box has 10 balls in it.
How many balls are there altogether?

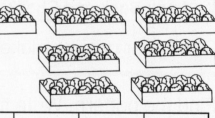

Number of Boxes							
Number of Balls							

The boxes have _____ balls in all.

Before, After, and Between

First find 34 on the chart.

1	2	3	4	5	6	7	8	9	10
11	12	13	14	15	16	17	18	19	20
21	22	23	24	25	26	27	28	29	30
31	32	33	(34)	35	36	37	38	39	40
41	42	43	44	45	46	47	48	49	50

Look to the left of 34 to find the number that comes before it.

_33_ comes **before** 34.

Look to the right of 34 to find the number that comes after it.

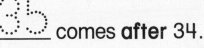 _35_ comes **after** 34.

 _34_ comes **between** 33 and 35.

Use Workmat 6 if you like.

Write the number that comes before.

1. _23_, 24   _____, 47   _____, 19

Write the number that comes after.

2. 32, _33_   41, _____   27, _____

Write the number that comes between.

3. 22, _____, 24   45, _____, 47   32, _____, 34

Problem Solving *Reasoning*

Write the number that answers the riddle.

4. I am a number between 10 and 20.
   You say my name when you count by 5s.

   What number am I? _____

Name _____

Before, After, and Between

Use Workmat 6 if you like.

Write the number that is just after.

1. 41, _42_   30, _____   59, _____

2. 85, _____   28, _____   63, _____

Write the number that is just before.

3. _____, 27   _____, 51   _____, 62

4. _____, 76   _____, 45   _____, 34

Write the numbers that are in between.

5. 21, _____, _____, 24   59, _____, _____, 62

6. 45, _____, _____, 48   73, _____, _____, 76

Problem Solving *Reasoning*

Write the number that answers the riddle.

7. I am between 40 and 50.

   You say my name when you count by fives.

   What number am I? _____

8. I am between 70 and 80.

   You say my name when you count by fives.

   What number am I? _____

Odd and Even Numbers

6 is an even number.
It makes equal rows.
There are no extras.

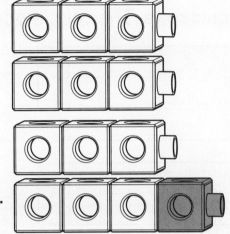

These cubes match.

7 is an odd number.
It does not make equal rows.
There is 1 extra.

These cubes don't match.

Use cubes to show each number.
Try to make equal rows.
Then circle **odd** or **even**.

1.

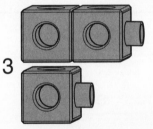

3

(odd)

even

2.

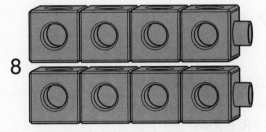

8

odd

even

3.

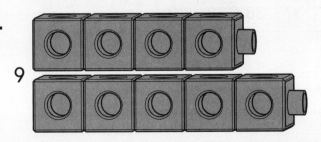

9

odd

even

Name _____

Odd and Even Numbers

Draw counters to show each number.
Try to make equal rows. Then circle **odd** or **even**.

1. 8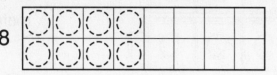

odd

(even)

2. 7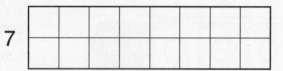

odd

even

3. 15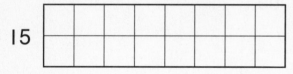

odd

even

4. 16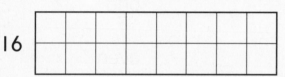

odd

even

Problem Solving *Visual Thinking*

5. Find the pattern.

   Write **odd** or **even** to complete each sentence.

21	22	23	24	25	26	27	28	29	30
31	32	33	34	35	36	37	38	39	40

   The shaded numbers are _____.

   The white numbers are _____.

Ordinal Numbers Through Twentieth

Ordinal numbers tell position.

1st 2nd 3rd 4th 5th 6th 7th 8th 9th 10th

↑ This girl is 1st in line.   ↑ This boy is 6th in line.

Follow the directions to show the position of the flowers.

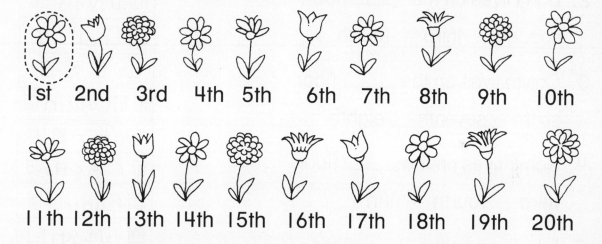

1st 2nd 3rd 4th 5th 6th 7th 8th 9th 10th

11th 12th 13th 14th 15th 16th 17th 18th 19th 20th

1. Circle the 1st flower in blue.

2. Circle the 10th flower in red.

3. Cross out the 18th flower.

4. Circle the 12th flower in yellow.

5. Draw a box around the flower that is 15th.

6. Circle the 5th flower in green.

Ordinal Numbers Through Twentieth

1. Circle the child who is sixth in line.

   Cross out the child who is ninth in line.

   Draw a square around the child who is second in line.

| 10th | 9th | 8th | 7th | 6th | 5th | 4th | 3rd | 2nd | 1st |
| tenth | ninth | eighth | seventh | sixth | fifth | fourth | third | second | first |

Circle the word that completes each sentence.

first
1st

2. Banji lives on the _____ floor.

   second   third   fourth

3. Calvin lives on the _____ floor.

   sixth   seventh   eighth

4. Samir lives on the _____ floor.

   third   fourth   fifth

5. Nan lives on the _____ floor.

   eighth   ninth   tenth

Problem Solving *Reasoning*

6.

   first second third fourth

   ?

   seventh eighth

   How many medals are missing? _____

PROBLEM-SOLVING APPLICATIONS

By the Sea

You can skip count to find out how many.

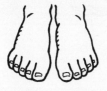 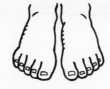 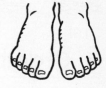

How many toes? Skip count by fives.
Add 5 to each number to get the next number.

_5_, _10_, _15_, _20_, _25_, _30_

1. Each boat has 2 sails. If there are 5 boats in all, skip count to find how many sails there are.

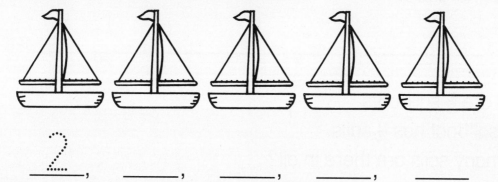

_2_, _____, _____, _____, _____

2. Is there an odd or even number of boats?

odd   even

3.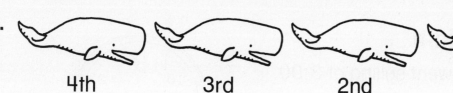

4th   3rd   2nd   1st

Circle the 1st whale.
Color the 3rd whale blue.

PROBLEM-SOLVING APPLICATIONS

By the Sea

1st

1. Circle the 2nd sailboat.

2. Draw a box around the 7th sailboat.

3. Is there an even or an odd number of sailboats?

even   odd

4. 5 people work on each sailboat. If there are
8 sailboats in all, skip count to find how many
people there are.

_____, _____, _____, _____, _____, _____, _____, _____

5. There are 6 sailboats.
Each sailboat has 4 sails.
How many sails are there in all?

Number of Sailboats					
Number of Sails					

Writing in Math

6. The family went sailing at 3:00.
They sailed for 3 hours.
Draw hands to show what time
the family returned from sailing.

Numbers Made with Tens

You can count the models to find out
how many groups of ten.

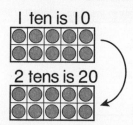

1 ten is 10

2 tens is 20

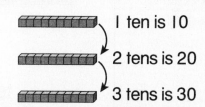

1 ten is 10

2 tens is 20

3 tens is 30

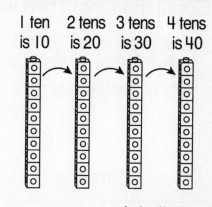

| 1 ten is 10 | 2 tens is 20 | 3 tens is 30 | 4 tens is 40 |

2 tens is _20_ .   3 tens is _30_ .   4 tens is _40_ .

Count the models. Write how many. Then write the number.

1. _1_ ten is _10_

_2_ tens is _20_

_3_ tens is _30_

_3_ tens is _30_ .

2. ____ ten is ____

____ tens is ____

____ tens is ____

____ tens is ____

_4_ tens is ____ .

3.

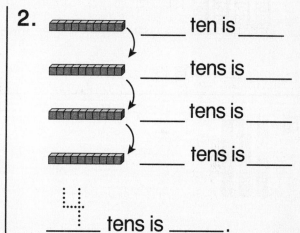

____ ten is ____

____ tens is ____

____ tens is ____

____ tens is ____

____ tens is ____

____ tens is ____ .

Numbers Made with Tens

Count the tens. Then write the numbers.

1. __5__ tens is __50__.

2. _____ tens is _____.

3. _____ tens is _____.

4. _____ tens is _____.

5. _____ tens is _____.

6. _____ tens is _____.

Problem Solving *Mental Math*

7. Nancy has 50 marbles.
   30 of the marbles are in one bag.
   The rest are in the second bag.
   How many marbles are in the
   second bag?

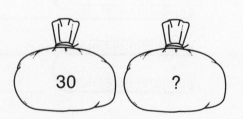

_____

Tens and Ones

Here are some ways you can show a number.

Tens	Ones

Tens	Ones
2	3

2 tens 3 ones

23

2 tens 3 ones

23

2 tens 3 ones

23

Count the tens and ones. Then write the numbers.

I.

Tens	Ones

3 tens 2 ones

3 tens 2 ones

32

32

32

2.

Tens	Ones

Tens	Ones

_____ tens _____ ones   _____ tens _____ ones   _____

_____   _____

Tens and Ones

Count the tens and ones. Then write the numbers.

1.

Tens	Ones

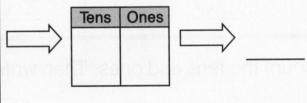

Tens	Ones
4	5

45

2.

Tens	Ones

Tens	Ones

_____

3.

Tens	Ones

Tens	Ones

_____

Problem Solving *Visual Thinking*

4. Javier wants to show 66 with models. Draw the
missing models to help Javier show 66.

Modeling Numbers and Expanded Form

The chart shows

Tens	Ones

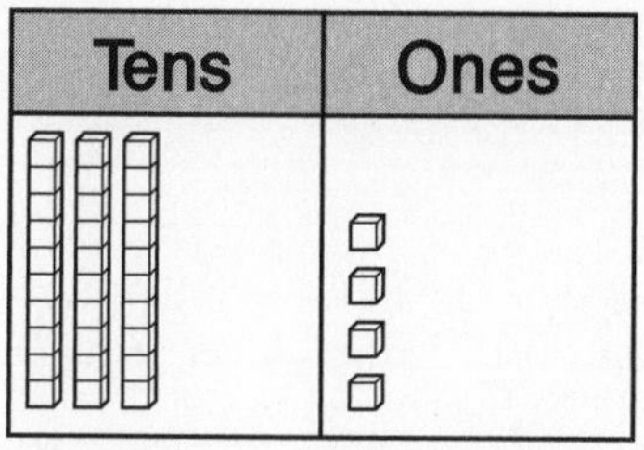

3 tens   4 ones

3 tens is 30
4 ones is 4
30 + 4 = 34

34 is the same as
3 tens and 4 ones.

Count the tens and ones. Then write the numbers.

1.

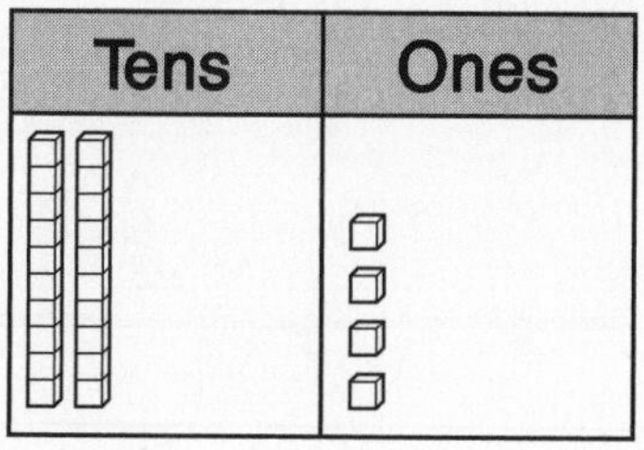

Tens	Ones

_2_ tens and _4_ ones

_2_ tens is _20_
_4_ ones is _4_
_20_ + _4_ = _24_

2.

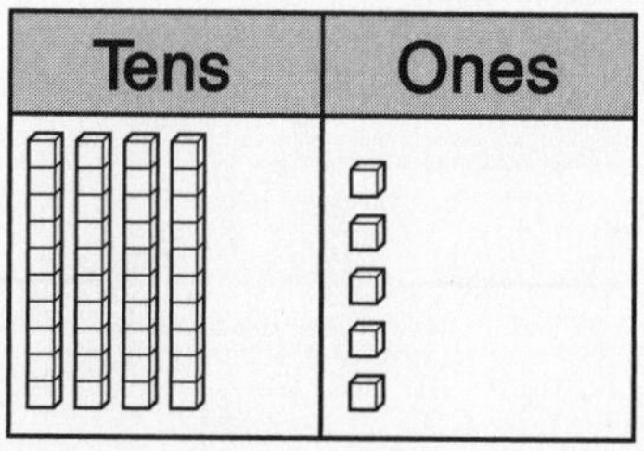 Tens	Ones

_____ tens and _____ ones

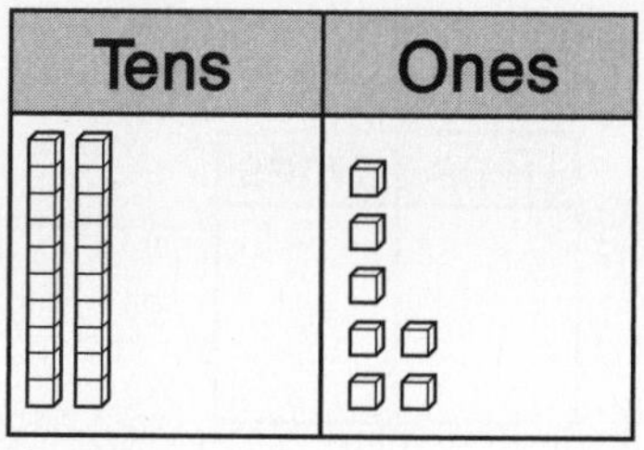

_____ tens is _____
_____ ones is _____
_____ + _____ = _____

3.

Tens	Ones

_____ tens and _____ ones

_____ tens is _____
_____ ones is _____
_____ + _____ = _____

Expanded Form

Draw the tens and ones. Then write the numbers.

1.

(36)

Tens	Ones

___3___ tens + ___6___ ones = __36__

__30__ + __6__ = __36__

2.

(54)

Tens	Ones

_____ tens + _____ ones = _____

_____ + _____ = _____

3.

(69)

Tens	Ones

_____ tens + _____ ones = _____

_____ + _____ = _____

Problem Solving *Reasoning*

Write the number that matches the clues.

4. The digit in the tens place is even,
and it is greater than 6.
The digit in the ones place is odd,
and it is between 3 and 7.

Tens	Ones

Ways to Make Numbers

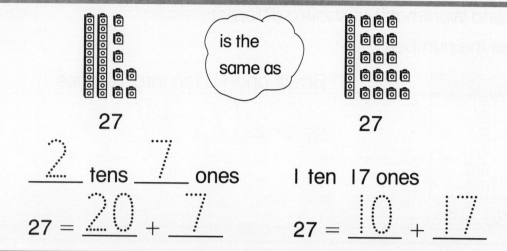

27

__2__ tens __7__ ones

27 = __20__ + __7__

27

I ten 17 ones

27 = __10__ + __17__

Use cubes and Workmat 4 to show a different way to make the number. Draw the ones.

1.   32

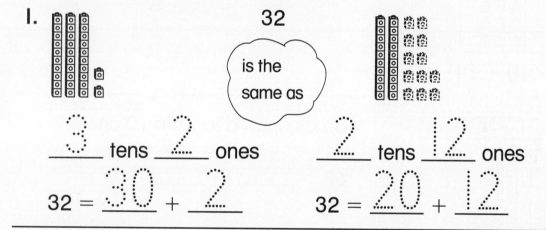

is the same as

__3__ tens __2__ ones

32 = __30__ + __2__

__2__ tens __12__ ones

32 = __20__ + __12__

2.

is the same as

_____ tens _____ ones

43 = _____ + _____

_____ tens _____ ones

43 = _____ + _____

Ways to Make Numbers

Use cubes and Workmat 4 to show a different
way to make the number.

1.

Tens	Ones

$37 = 30 + 7$

Break apart a ten into 10 ones.

$37 = \underline{20} + \underline{17}$

2.

Tens	Ones

$24 = 10 + 14$

Make a ten with 10 ones.

$24 = \underline{} + \underline{}$

3.

Tens	Ones

$62 = 60 + 2$

Break apart a ten into 10 ones.

$62 = \underline{} + \underline{}$

Problem Solving *Number Sense*

Use cubes to solve. Circle **yes** or **no**.

4. On Mario's workmat there are
4 tens and 8 ones. On Jeb's
workmat there are 3 tens and
18 ones. Are the boys showing
the same number on their workmats?

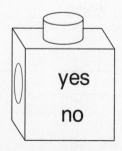

yes

no

Use Objects

Jo has 11 red balloons and 13 blue balloons.
How many balloons does she have in all?

Read and Understand

You need to find how many balloons Jo has in all.

Plan and Solve

Make each number with cubes.

Put the cubes together.
Join the tens. Join the ones.

There are __2__ tens and __4__ ones.

Jo has __24__ balloons.

11 and 13

is

20 and 4

Look Back and Check

How can you check that your amount is correct?

Use cubes to find how many in all.

1. Dan has 22 books. Mike has 13 books.
   How many books do they have in all?

   There are _____ tens and _____ ones.

   They have _____ books in all.

PROBLEM SOLVING STRATEGY

Use Objects

Use cubes to find how many there are in all.

1. How many potatoes are there in all?

   potatoes   potatoes

   36 potatoes

2. How many apples are there in all?

   apples   apples

   _____ apples

3. How many tomatoes are there in all?

   tomatoes   tomatoes

   _____ tomatoes

4. How many oranges are there in all?

   oranges   oranges

   _____ oranges

Problem Solving *Algebra*

Use cubes. Write the number
of bananas below the basket.

5. There are 37 bananas in all.
   21 bananas are in one basket.
   How many bananas are there
   in the other basket?

   21 bananas   _____ bananas

1 More, 1 Less;
10 More, 10 Less

34 take away 10 is 24.

10 less than 34 is __24__.

34 and 10 more is 44.

10 more than 34 is __44__.

Use cubes. Write the numbers.

1.

23 take away 1 is __22__.

1 less than 23 is _____.

23 and 1 more is __24__.

1 more than 23 is _____.

2.

1 less than 45 is _____.

1 more than 45 is _____.

3.

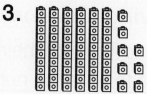

10 less than 68 is _____.

10 more than 68 is _____.

1 More, 1 Less;
10 More, 10 Less

Use cubes. Write the numbers.

1.

1 more than 35 is _36_.

10 less than 35 is _25_.

2.

10 more than 26 is _____.

1 less than 26 is _____.

3.

10 less than 42 is _____.

1 more than 42 is _____.

4.

1 less than 70 is _____.

10 more than 70 is _____.

Problem Solving *Reasoning*

5. Stan, Don, and Tom got their team shirts.
Use the clues to write the number of each boy's shirt.
The number on Stan's shirt is 10 less than Don's.
The number on Don's shirt is 1 more than Tom's.
Tom's number is 16.

_____   _____   _____
Stan   Don   Tom

© Pearson Education, Inc. 1

Comparing Numbers: Greater Than, Less Than, Equal

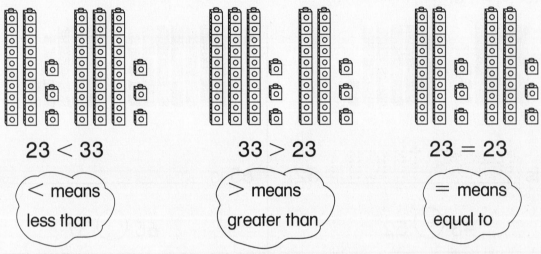

$$23 < 33 \qquad\qquad 33 > 23 \qquad\qquad 23 = 23$$

< means
less than

> means
greater than

= means
equal to

23 is **less than** 33   33 is **greater than** 23   23 is **equal to** 23

Circle **less than**, **greater than**, or **equal to**.

Write <, >, or =.

1. 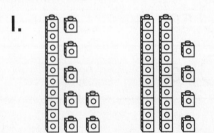   (less than)   greater than   equal to

17 ◁ 24

2.   less than   greater than   equal to

45 ◯ 32

3.   less than   greater than   equal to

29 ◯ 29

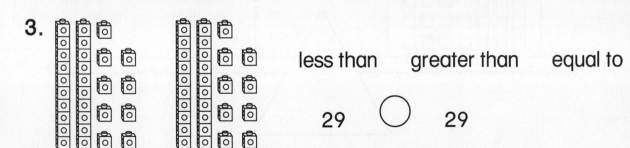

Comparing Numbers: Greater Than, Less Than, Equal

Write <, >, or =.

1.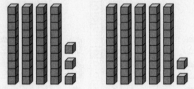

43 is 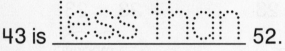 _less than_ 52.

43 < 52

2.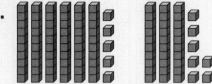

65 is _____ 37.

65 ◯ 37

| < less than | > greater than | = equal to |

Write <, >, or =.

3. 27 ◯ 27

4. 45 ◯ 50

5. 59 ◯ 41

6. 35 ◯ 53

Problem Solving *Visual Thinking*

7. Draw different models in the empty box.
   Make both sides equal.

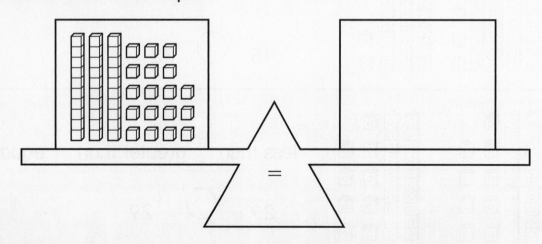

Number-Line Estimation: Numbers to 100

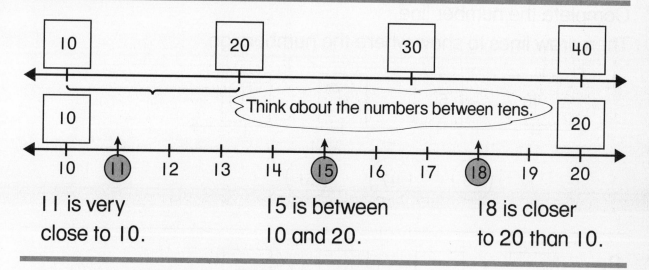

| 10 | 20 | 30 | 40 |

Think about the numbers between tens.

| 10 | | 20 |

10   11   12   13   14   15   16   17   18   19   20

11 is very close to 10.

15 is between 10 and 20.

18 is closer to 20 than 10.

Count by tens to complete the number line.
Then draw lines to show where the numbers go.

1.

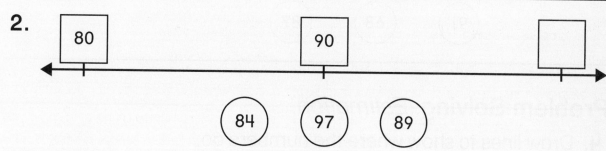

| 50 | 60 | 70 |

62   55   68

2.

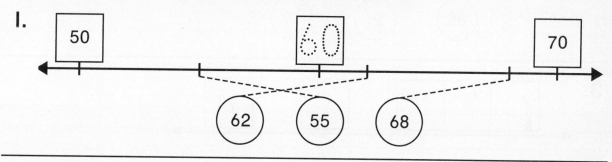

| 80 | 90 | |

84   97   89

3.

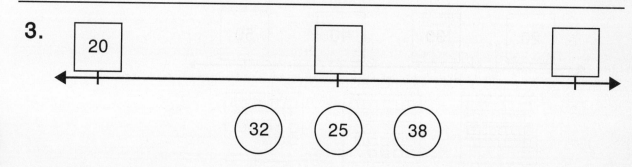

| 20 | | |

32   25   38

Number-Line Estimation: Numbers to 100

Complete the number line.

Then draw lines to show where the numbers go.

1.

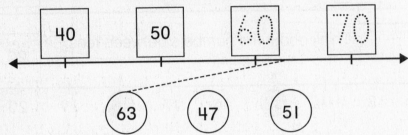

2.

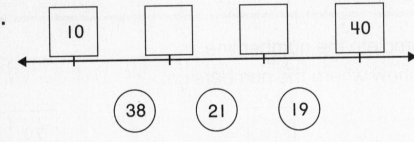

3.

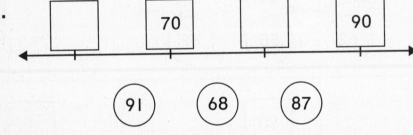

Problem Solving *Estimation*

4. Draw lines to show where the numbers go.

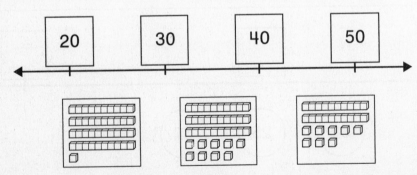

Ordering Three Numbers

The number line can help you put numbers in order.

Show (27) (14) (38) from **least** to **greatest**.

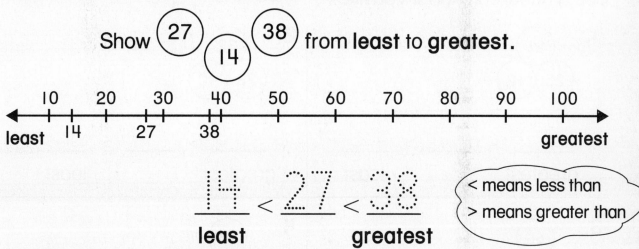

14 < 27 < 38
least   greatest

< means less than
> means greater than

Write the numbers in order from **least** to **greatest**.

1.

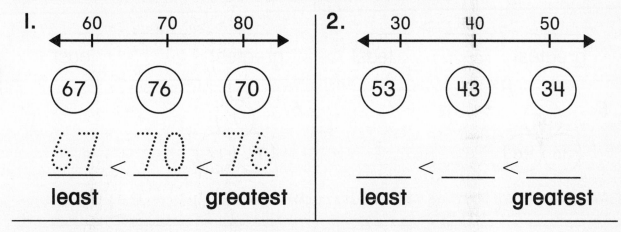

67 < 70 < 76
least   greatest

2.

___ < ___ < ___
least   greatest

Write the numbers in order from **greatest** to **least**.
Use the number line to help you.

3.

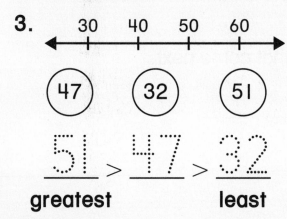

51 > 47 > 32
greatest   least

4.

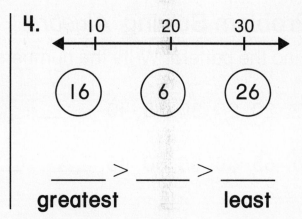

___ > ___ > ___
greatest   least

Ordering Three Numbers

Write the numbers in order from **greatest** to **least**.
Use a hundred chart if you like.

1.

(21)
(25)(12)

25 > 21 > 12
greatest   least

2.

(32)
(23)(40)

_____ > _____ > _____
greatest   least

3.

(60)
(56)(65)

_____ > _____ > _____
greatest   least

4.

(16)
(6)(26)

_____ > _____ > _____
greatest   least

5.

(62)
(36)(46)

_____ > _____ > _____
greatest   least

6.

(7)
(71)(17)

_____ > _____ > _____
greatest   least

Problem Solving *Algebra*

Find the pattern. Write the numbers that come next.

7. 20, 25, 30, 35, 40, _____, _____, _____

8. 65, 60, 55, 50, 45, _____, _____, _____

Hundreds

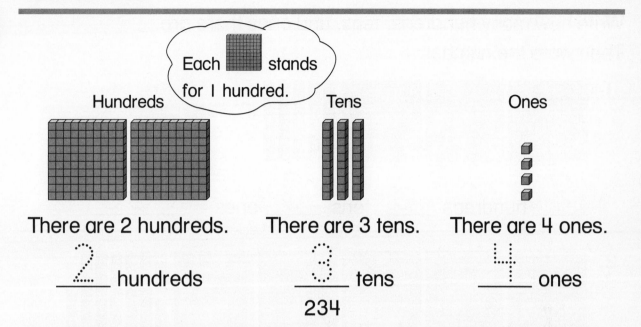

Each ▦ stands for 1 hundred.

Hundreds

There are 2 hundreds.

__2__ hundreds

Tens

There are 3 tens.

__3__ tens

234

Ones

There are 4 ones.

__4__ ones

Write how many hundreds, tens, and ones there are.
Then write the number.

1.

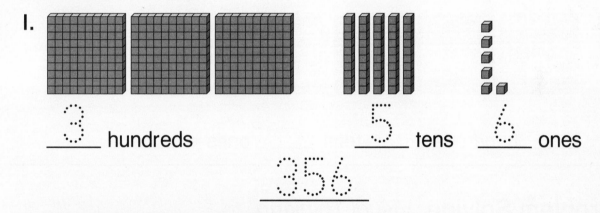

__3__ hundreds

__5__ tens   __6__ ones

356

2.

_____ hundreds

_____ tens   _____ ones

_____

Hundreds

Write how many hundreds, tens, and ones there are.
Then write the number.

1.

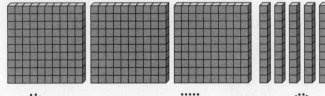

___3___ hundreds ___5___ tens ___0___ ones = ___350___

2.

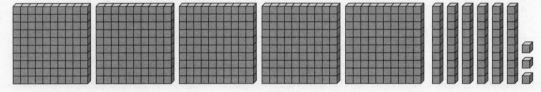

_____ hundreds _____ tens _____ ones = _____

3.

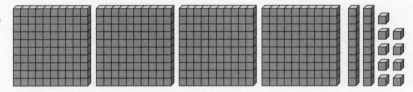

_____ hundreds _____ tens _____ ones = _____

Problem Solving *Visual Thinking*

4. Write the missing numbers in the chart.

491				495		497		499	
	502	503				507			510
511			514					519	
521		523		525				529	530

Sorting

Sort these squares and circles in two different ways.

By Size	By Color

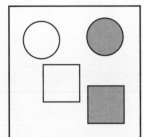 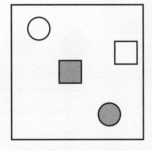 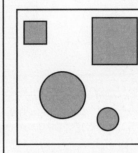 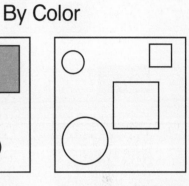

| These squares and circles are <u>big</u>. | These squares and circles are <u>small</u>. | These squares and circles are <u>gray</u>. | These squares and circles are <u>white</u>. |

1. Sort the squares and circles another way.
   Tell the way that you sorted.

These are all <u>squares</u>.   These are all _____.

I sorted by _____.

Problem Solving *Reasoning*

2. Circle the shape that does not belong in the group.

Sorting

How could you sort these shapes?
Draw and color to show two groups you could make.

1.

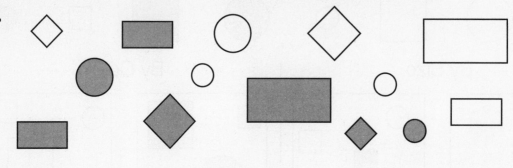

Problem Solving *Reasoning*

Circle the shape that does not belong in the group.

2.

Making Graphs

Each flower is 1 selection.

Favorite Flower

Daisy 🌼	🌼	🌼	🌼	🌼	🌼	🌼	🌼			
Tulip 🌷	🌷	🌷	🌷	🌷						

Count the pictures in the graph.

How many boxes have a daisy? ___7___

How many boxes have a tulip? ___4___

Which flower is the favorite? ___Daisy___

1. Ask your classmates to select their favorite drink.
   Draw to make a picture graph.

Our Favorite Drink

Apple Juice 🍎										
Milk 🥛										

2. What will you draw to show apple juice? __🍎__

3. What will you draw to show milk? _____

4. How many children selected apple juice? _____

5. Which drink is the least favorite? _____

Making Graphs

1. Ask your class to select their favorite snack.
   Draw to make a picture graph.
   Then answer the questions.

Our Favorite Snacks		

Pizza	Peanuts	Popcorn

2. Which snack is the
   favorite of the class?

   _____

3. Which snack is the
   least favorite?

   _____

4. How many children would
   have selected pizza if
   2 more children had selected it?

   _____

Problem Solving *Writing in Math*

5. Write a question about the picture graph above.

   _____

   _____

Making Bar Graphs

Each square that is colored gray equals 1 child's selection.

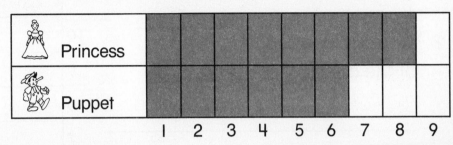

Names of Fairy-Tale Characters

Look at the number of squares colored for the princess.

How many squares are colored? __8__

Number of selections

Look at the number of squares colored for the puppet.

How many squares are colored? __6__

Circle the favorite fairy-tale character of the children.

(Princess)   Puppet

1. Ask your classmates to select their favorite snack.
   Color to make a bar graph. Then answer the questions.

Yogurt									
Fruit									

   1   2   3   4   5   6   7   8   9

2. Which snack is the favorite? _____

3. How many children selected fruit? _____

Making Bar Graphs

1. Ask your classmates to select their favorite sticker.
   Color to make a bar graph.
   Then answer the questions.

Our Favorite Stickers		
10		
9		
8		
7		
6		
5		
4		
3		
2		
1		
Flowers	Birds	Dinosaurs

2. Which sticker is the favorite
   of the class?

   _____

3. Which sticker is the
   least favorite?

   _____

4. How many children would
   have selected the bird sticker
   if 1 more child had selected it?

   _____

Problem Solving *Number Sense*

5. Put the stickers in order from **least** to **greatest**
   according to the number of spaces colored.
   Write the words **Flowers, Birds,** and **Dinosaurs.**

   _____ , _____ , _____

       least   **greatest**

Using Tally Marks

The children made tally marks to show the ways children get to school.

| equals I

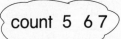equals 5

(count 5 6 7)

		Total
Walk	卌 ||	7
School bus	卌 卌	10

(count 5   10)

---

1. Color some balloons red. Color the rest blue.
   Use tally marks to show how many balloons
   there are in each color. Write the totals.

		Total
Red		
Blue		

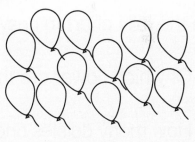

Use the tally chart to answer the questions.

2. Of which color are there the most? _____

3. Of which color are there the fewest? _____

4. How many balloons are there altogether? _____

Using Tally Marks

Write tally marks to show how many flowers
there are of each kind. Write the totals.

		Total
Rose		
Tulip		
Daisy		

Use the tally chart to answer the questions.

1. Of which flower are there the fewest? _____

2. How many daisies and roses are there altogether? _____

3. How many more daisies than tulips are there? _____

Problem Solving *Writing in Math*

4. Write your own question about the tally chart above.

_____

_____

Coordinate Grids

This is a map of Felipe's town.

You want to go from the school to Felipe's house.

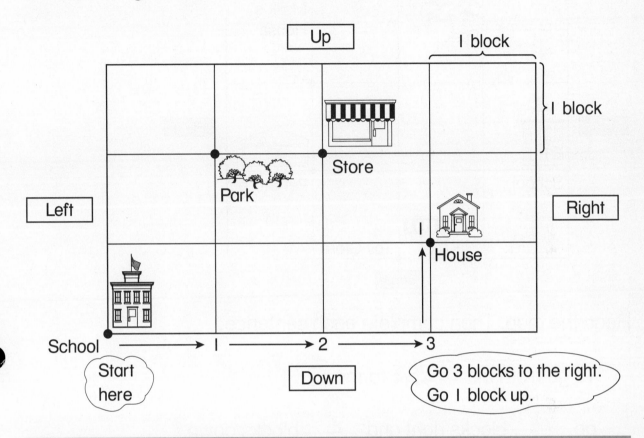

Read the map. Then complete each sentence.

1. To go from the 🏫 to the 🌳 ,

   go _____ block right and _2_ blocks up.

---

2. To go from the 🏫 to the 🏪 ,

   go _____ block left and _____ block up.

---

3. To go from the 🏫 to the 🌳 ,

   go _____ blocks left and _____ block up.

Name ____________________

Coordinate Grids

This is a map of Malik's town.

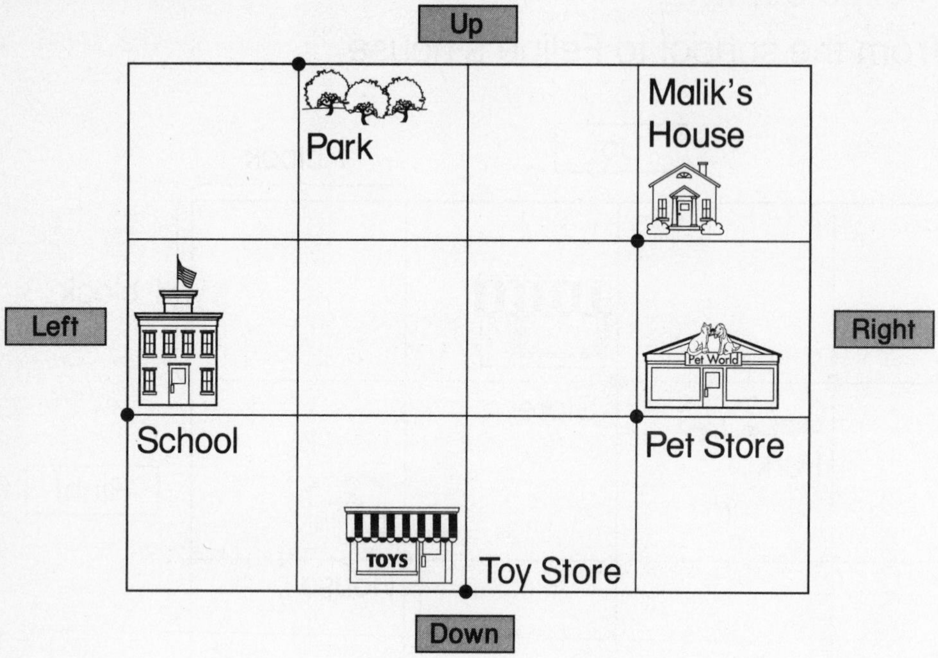

Read the map. Then complete each sentence.

1. To go from the 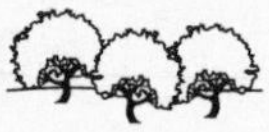 to the 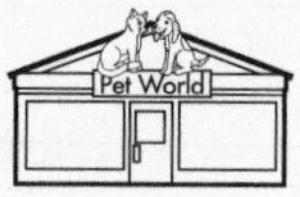,

   go 2 blocks right and 2 blocks down.

2. To go from the 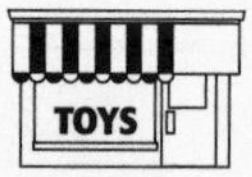 to the 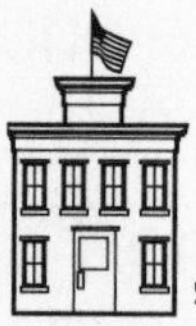,

   go ____ blocks left and ____ block up.

Problem Solving *Visual Thinking*

3. Start at the .
   Move 4 spaces to the left
   and 1 space down.
   Draw a circle.

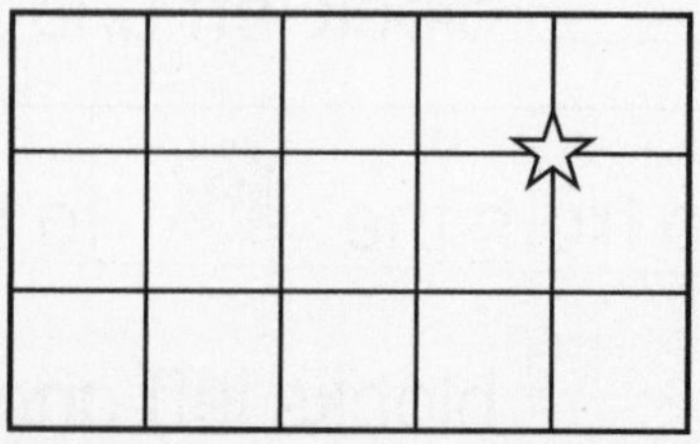

Use Data from a Map

This is a map of a neighborhood.
How many blocks is it from the house to the park?

Step 1:
You need to find out how many blocks in all.

Step 2:
Look at the map.
Find the house.
Find the park.

From house to store __3__ blocks.

From store to park __2__ blocks.

Library *2 blocks* *School*
4 blocks *3 blocks* *3 blocks*
Park
2 blocks
Store *3 blocks* *House*

Step 3:
Write an addition sentence.

__3__ + __2__ = __5__ blocks

It is 5 blocks from the house to the park.

I. How many blocks is it from the park to the school?
Find the shortest path. Write an addition sentence.

From the 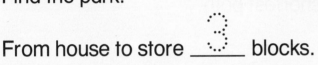 to the _____ _____ blocks

From the _____ to the _____ _____ blocks

_____ + _____ = _____ blocks

Name _____

Use Data from a Map

Green Park

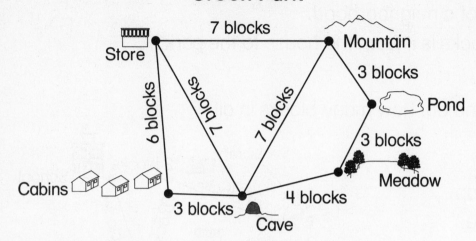

How many blocks is it? Find the shortest path.
Then write an addition sentence.

1. From the 🏠🏠🏠 to the ⛰

   __3__ + __7__ = __10__ blocks

2. From the ☁ to the 🏪

   _____ + _____ = _____ blocks

3. From the 🏠🏠🏠 to the 🌳🌳

   _____ + _____ = _____ blocks

4. From the ⛰ to the ☁

   _____ + _____ = _____ blocks

5. From the ⛰ to the 🌳🌳

   _____ + _____ = _____ blocks

PROBLEM-SOLVING APPLICATIONS R 8-17

Let's Make Soup!

Count the striped fish. Make 1 tally mark for each striped fish. Count the dotted fish. Make 1 tally mark for each dotted fish. Write the totals.

Remember ||||| equals 5.

		Total
striped fish	IIII III	
dotted fish	IIII II	

Look back and check.

Count the striped fish again. How many are there? __8__
Count the tally marks for striped fish.

What is the total? __8__

Are the numbers the same? __yes__

1. How many dotted fish did you count? _____

2. How many dotted fish are on the tally chart? _____

3. How many fewer dotted fish are there than striped fish? _____

4. Circle the picture that shows what you wrote on the tally chart.

 <    >

Name ______________________________

Let's Make Soup!

1. Make tally marks to show how many of each vehicle there are. Then write the totals.

Car 		
Bus 		
Truck 		

2. Write the numbers of vehicles in order from **least** to **greatest**.

_____ < _____ < _____

least **greatest**

Writing in Math

3. Make a picture graph that shows how many of each vehicle are on this page.

Nickel and Penny

A nickel = 5 cents.
Skip count by 5s for nickels.

A penny = 1 cent.
Count by 1s for pennies.

Skip count by 5s for the nickels.
Then count on by 1s for the pennies.

5¢ → 10¢ → 15¢ → 16¢ → 17¢ → 18¢

In All

18¢

Skip count by 5s and count on by 1s to find
how much money in all.

1.

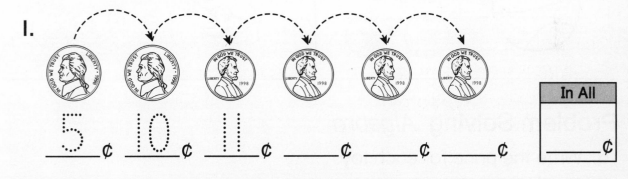

5¢ 10¢ 11¢ ____¢ ____¢ ____¢

In All

____¢

2.

____¢ ____¢ ____¢ ____¢ ____¢ ____¢

In All

____¢

Name _____

Nickel and Penny

Count on. Then write how much money in all.

1.

5₵ 6₵ 7₵ 8₵ 9₵

In All
9 ₵

2.

_____₵ _____₵ _____₵ _____₵ _____₵

In All
_____ ₵

Circle the coins that match each price.

3. 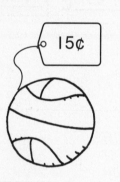 15₵

4.  13₵

Problem Solving *Algebra*

5. Write the price for each toy.
Remember, the price of the
sailboat must stay the same.

Together, these toys cost 10₵.

_____ ₵   _____ ₵

Together, these toys cost 8₵.

_____ ₵   _____ ₵

Dime

A dime = 10 cents.
Skip count by 10s for dimes.

A penny = 1 cent.
Count by 1s for pennies.

Skip count by 10s. Then count on by 1s.

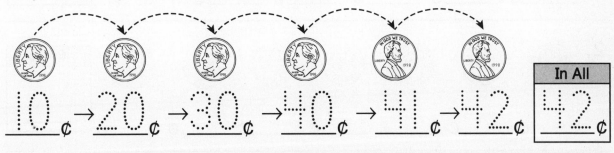

10¢ → 20¢ → 30¢ → 40¢ → 41¢ → 42¢

In All

42¢

Skip count by 10s and count on by 1s to find
how much money in all.

1.

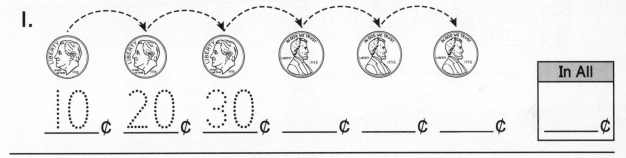

10¢ 20¢ 30¢ _____¢ _____¢ _____¢

In All

_____¢

2.

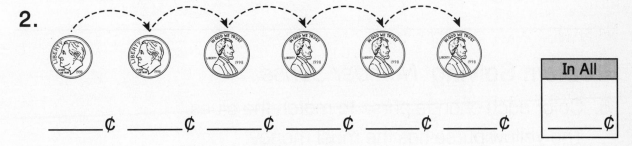

_____¢ _____¢ _____¢ _____¢ _____¢ _____¢

In All

_____¢

Dime

Count on. Then write how much money in all.

1.

10¢ 20¢ 30¢ 31¢ 32¢

In All

32¢

2.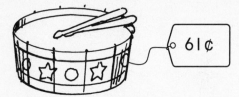

___¢ ___¢ ___¢ ___¢ ___¢ ___¢ ___¢

In All

___¢

Circle the coins that match each price.

3.  61¢

4.  33¢

Problem Solving *Number Sense*

5. Color each change purse to match the clues.

The yellow purse has the most money.

The blue purse has more money than the orange purse.

Counting Dimes and Nickels

Count dimes by 10s.   Count nickels by 5s.

Count the dimes first.   Then count the nickels.

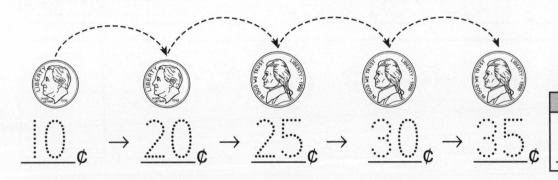

$$10_¢ \rightarrow 20_¢ \rightarrow 25_¢ \rightarrow 30_¢ \rightarrow 35_¢$$

In All
$35_¢$

Count on. Then write how much money in all.

1.

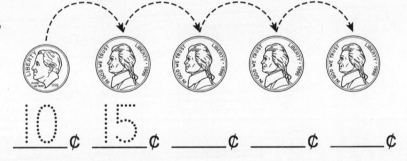

$$10_¢ \quad 15_¢ \quad \underline{}_¢ \quad \underline{}_¢ \quad \underline{}_¢$$

In All
___¢

2.

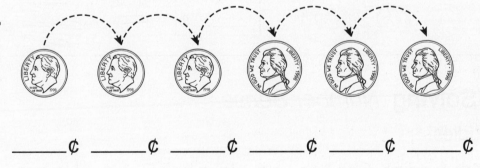

$$\underline{}_¢ \quad \underline{}_¢ \quad \underline{}_¢ \quad \underline{}_¢ \quad \underline{}_¢ \quad \underline{}_¢$$

In All
___¢

Counting Dimes and Nickels

Count on. Then write how much money in all.

1.

10¢ 20¢ 25¢ 30¢ 35¢ 40¢

In All
40¢

2.

___¢ ___¢ ___¢ ___¢ ___¢ ___¢ ___¢

In All
___¢

Write how much money in all.
Then circle the toy that you can buy.

3.

In All
60¢

 65¢

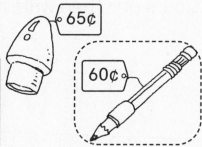 60¢

4.

In All
___¢

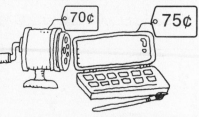 70¢ 75¢

Problem Solving *Number Sense*

Solve the riddles.

5. Hayes has 5 coins. She has 2 dimes. The rest are nickels. How much money does Hayes have?

____¢

6. Jake has 5 coins. He has 2 nickels. The rest are dimes. How much money does Jake have?

____¢

Counting Dimes, Nickels, and Pennies   **R 9-4**

When you count coins, start with the coin that is worth the most.

A dime is worth more than a nickel.
A nickel is worth more than a penny.

Count dimes by 10s.   Count nickels by 5s.   Count pennies by 1s.

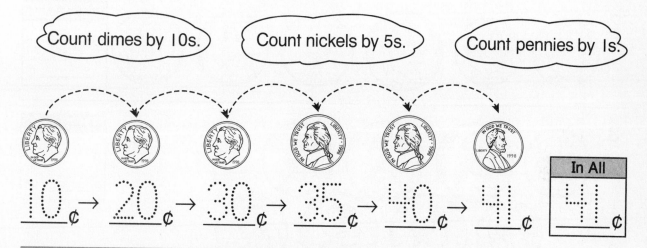

10¢ → 20¢ → 30¢ → 35¢ → 40¢ → 41¢   **In All** 41¢

Count on. Then write how much money in all.

1.

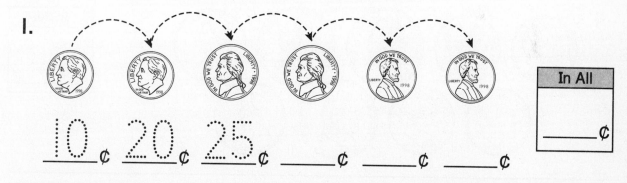

10¢ 20¢ 25¢ ____¢ ____¢ ____¢   **In All** ____¢

2.

____¢ ____¢ ____¢ ____¢ ____¢ ____¢   **In All** ____¢

Counting Dimes, Nickels, and Pennies

Count on. Then write how much money in all.

1.

In All
37 ¢

2.

In All
_____ ¢

3.

In All
_____ ¢

4.

In All
_____ ¢

Problem Solving *Algebra*

5. There are five coins in Dan's bank.
   Some are dimes, and some are nickels.
   What is the greatest amount
   of money Dan could have? _____ ¢
   What is the least amount
   of money Dan could have? _____ ¢

Use Data from a Table

Meg buys a top.
She gives the clerk a dime.
Will she get change?

Toys		
Top	(top)	9¢
Ball	(ball)	7¢
Jacks	(jacks)	5¢

The price of the toy is on the same line as the toy.

Find the top in the table.
How much is a top?

A top is __9__ ¢.

Read the story again.
How much money did Meg give the clerk?

Meg gave the clerk __a dime__.

A dime is 10¢.

10¢ is more than 9¢.

Will Meg get change? __yes__

Use the table above. Circle **yes** or **no**.

You Buy	You Use	Will you get change?
I. (ball)	(nickel) (penny) (penny)	yes no
2. (jacks)	(dime)	yes no

Use Data from a Table

Use the menu. Write **yes** or **no**.

Menu

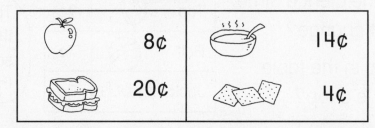

You Buy	You Use	Will you get change?
I. 🥣	🪙 🪙 🪙	
2. 🥪	🪙 🪙 🪙	
3. 🍎	🪙 🪙 🪙 🪙	

Problem Solving *Writing in Math*

4. Write a story problem using information from the menu.

_____

_____

_____

Quarter

There are different ways you can make 25 cents.

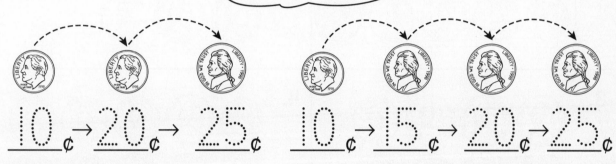

Skip count by 10s and then by 5s.

$$10_\text{¢} \rightarrow 20_\text{¢} \rightarrow 25_\text{¢} \qquad 10_\text{¢} \rightarrow 15_\text{¢} \rightarrow 20_\text{¢} \rightarrow 25_\text{¢}$$

Count each group of coins.
Circle the group of coins in each row that equals 25 cents.

1.

2.

3.

Problem Solving *Visual Thinking*

4. Chris has 4 coins in her purse.
They are worth 25¢ in all.
Draw the other 2 coins.

Quarter

Circle the coins that equal 25¢.

1.

2.

3.

4.

5.

Problem Solving *Visual Thinking*

6. Lucia has 4 coins in her purse.
   They are worth 25¢ in all.
   Draw and label Lucia's coins.

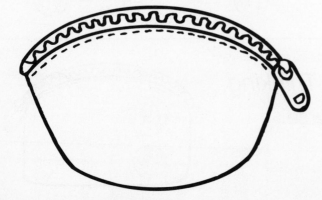

> > >

Remember > stands for greater than.

Count the coins. Start with the coin that is worth the most money.

Count on by 10s.   Count on by 5s.   Count on by 1s.

25¢ → 35¢ → 45¢ → 50¢ → 55¢ → 56¢ → 57¢

In All

57¢

Count on. Then write how much money in all.

1.

25¢ 35¢ ____¢ ____¢ ____¢ ____¢

In All

____¢

2.

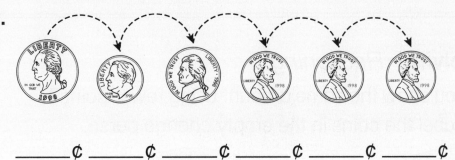

____¢ ____¢ ____¢ ____¢ ____¢ ____¢

In All

____¢

Counting Sets of Coins

Count on. Then write how much money in all.

1.

$\underline{25}_¢$ $\underline{35}_¢$ $\underline{40}_¢$ $\underline{45}_¢$ $\underline{50}_¢$ $\underline{51}_¢$ $\underline{52}_¢$

In All
$\underline{52}_¢$

2.

____¢ ____¢ ____¢ ____¢ ____¢ ____¢

In All
____¢

Circle the coins that match each amount.

3.

57¢

4.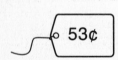

53¢

Problem Solving *Reasoning*

5. How can you show the same amount using fewer coins?
   Draw and label the coins in the empty change purse.

 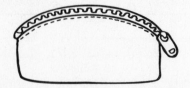

Half-Dollar and Dollar

Here are some ways to show one dollar.

dollar bill

$1.00 = 100¢

dollar coin

 or

$1.00 = 100¢

half-dollar coin

 or

half-dollar = 50¢
2 half-dollars = 100¢

4 quarters

25¢ → 50¢ → 75¢ → 100¢

4 quarters = 100¢

Circle the group of coins in each row that makes $1.00.

1.

2.

3.

Half-Dollar and Dollar

Write how much money in all.

1.

In All
$1.00

2.

In All
_____

3.

In All
_____

Problem Solving *Reasoning*

4. How can you show the same amount using only
2 coins? Draw and label the coins in the empty bank.

Try, Check, and Revise

Jim bought 2 toys at the toy fair. Together they cost 11¢.
Which toys did he buy?

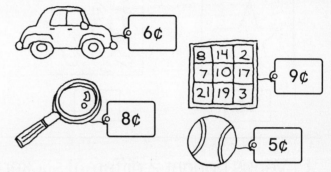

Read and Understand

Pick two toys. Find their total.

Plan and Solve

Try 🚗 and 🔍.

Add. __6__ ¢ + __8__ ¢ = __14__ ¢

> 14¢ is more than 11¢.

Find a toy that costs less than 🔍.

The ⚾ costs less.

Try the 🚗 and ⚾.

Add. __6__ ¢ + __5__ ¢ = __11__ ¢

Jim bought the 🚗 and ⚾.

Look Back and Check

How can you check your answer?

---

1. Circle the 2 toys that cost 15¢.

_____ ¢ + _____ ¢ = _____ ¢

Try, Check, and Revise

Circle the stickers each child bought.
Then write an addition sentence to check your guess.

4¢   5¢   9¢   8¢

---

1. Venus bought 2 different stickers.
   Together they cost 14¢.
   What did Venus buy?

_____ + _____ = _____ ¢

---

2. Carlos bought 2 different stickers.
   Together they cost 9¢.
   What did Carlos buy?

_____ + _____ = _____ ¢

---

3. Anita bought 2 different stickers.
   Together they cost 12¢.
   What did Anita buy?

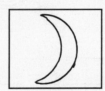 

 _____ + _____ = _____ ¢

What Can You Buy?

 8¢

Circle the coins you need to buy 1 bear.

Check your answer.

How much is the bear? __8__ ¢

Count the coins you circled.

How much are they worth? __8__ ¢

Do the coins equal the price of the bear? __yes__

---

1. Circle the coins you need to buy 2 bears.

---

2. Is the price of the 2 bears
an odd or even number? _____

---

3. Circle the coins you need to buy the puzzle.

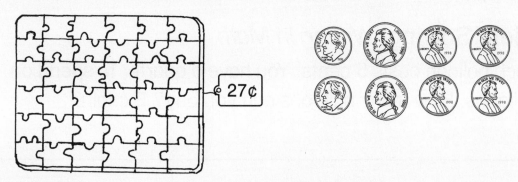 27¢

Name _____

What Can You Buy?

1. Circle the coins you need to buy 1 top.

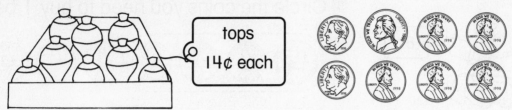

2. Circle the coins you need to buy 1 pencil.

3. Circle the coins you need to buy 2 pencils.

Write **less than** or **greater than.**

4. The price of a pencil is _____ the price of a top.

5. Is the price of a top an odd number
   or an even number? _____

Problem Solving *Writing in Math*

6. Each balloon costs 5 cents. You have a quarter to spend on
   balloons. How many balloons can you buy? Explain.

_____

Estimating, Measuring, and Comparing Length

Look at the paper clip.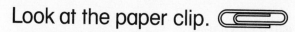

Look at the string. _____

Estimate: How many paper clips long is the string?

About __5__ paper clips long.

Now measure.

> Be sure you put the paper clips right next to each other.

> Be sure paper clips are all the same size.

> Line up the first paper clip with the edge.

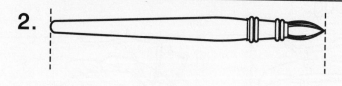

Measure: About __6__ paper clips long.
  That is close to the estimate.

Estimate. Then measure using paper clips.

	Estimate.	Measure.
1.	about _____ ⌖	_____ ⌖
2.	Estimate. about _____ ⌖	Measure. _____ ⌖
3.	Estimate. about _____ ⌖	Measure. _____ ⌖

Name _____

Estimating, Measuring, and Comparing Length

Find each object in your classroom.
Estimate the length. Then measure using cubes.

	Estimate.	Measure.
1. ERASER	about _____ 🔲	about _____ 🔲
2.	about _____ 🔲	about _____ 🔲
3.	about _____ 🔲	about _____ 🔲

Problem Solving *Visual Thinking*

4. Measure each bug using cubes. Circle the longest bug.
Mark an **X** on the shortest bug.

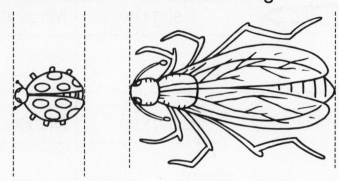

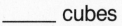 cube   _____ cubes   _____ cubes

Use Logical Reasoning

Predict: Will you need more chalk or
more paper clips to measure the marker?

more 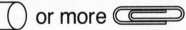 or more

Read and Understand

You must find out if you need more chalk or more paper clips.

Plan and Solve

Use reasoning to help you.

The paper clip is shorter.

You will probably need more paper clips.

more    (more paper clip)   Measure to check.

Look Back and Check

Measure to check your prediction.
Was your prediction correct?

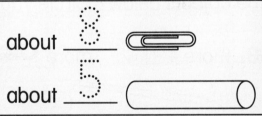

about ___8___ paper clip

about ___5___ chalk

Will it take fewer pieces of chalk or fewer paper clips?
Circle your prediction. Then measure.

I.
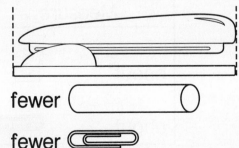

fewer (chalk)

fewer (paper clip)

Measure to check.

about _____ paper clip

about _____ chalk

© Pearson Education, Inc. 1

PROBLEM-SOLVING STRATEGY

Use Logical Reasoning

Will it take fewer snap cubes or fewer paper clips
to measure the objects below?
Circle your prediction. Then measure.

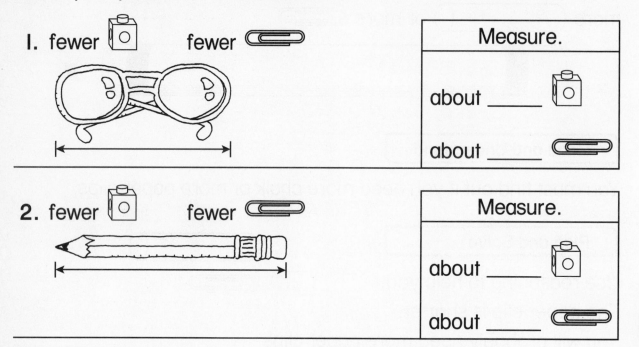

1. fewer 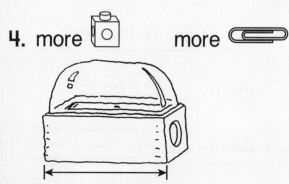 fewer ⬭

Measure.

about _____ 🔲

about _____ ⬭

2. fewer 🔲 fewer ⬭

Measure.

about _____ 🔲

about _____ ⬭

Will it take more snap cubes or more paper clips to measure
the objects below? Circle your prediction. Then measure.

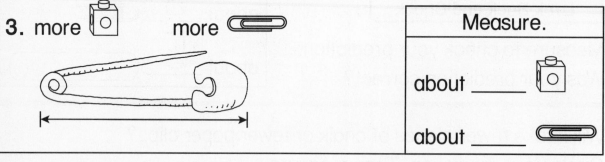

3. more 🔲 more ⬭

Measure.

about _____ 🔲

about _____ ⬭

4. more 🔲 more ⬭

Measure.

about _____ 🔲

about _____ ⬭

Estimating and Measuring with Inches   R 10-3

This is 1 inch. [ruler showing 1 inch]

About how
many inches
long is this ribbon?

About __6__ inches long.
Measure. Use a ruler.

Line up the edge
of the ribbon
with the edge of
the ruler.

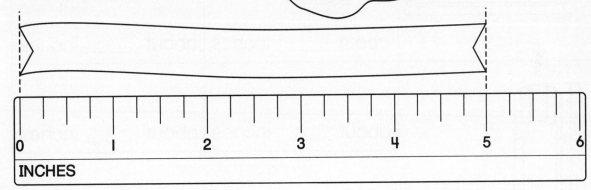

The ribbon measures __5__ inches long.
Was your estimate correct?

Estimate the length. Then measure using a ruler.

I. [ruler showing 1 inch]

Estimate.

Measure.

about _____ inches

_____ inches

Estimating and Measuring with Inches

Find each object in your classroom.
Estimate the length or height.
Then measure using a ruler.

	Estimate.	Measure.
1.	about _____ inches	about _____ inches
2.	about _____ inches	about _____ inches
3.	about _____ inches	about _____ inches

Problem Solving *Mental Math*

Answer the questions.

4. This stamp is 1 inch long.

   How long are 4 stamps? _____ inches

   How long are 6 stamps? _____ inches

Estimating and Measuring with Feet

A foot is 12 inches long.

This football is about 1 foot long.

An inch ruler is 1 foot long.

About how long is your desk?

about _____ feet long

You can use an inch ruler to measure the length of your desk.

Mark the place where your ruler ends.
Then start measuring again at that mark.

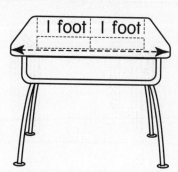

The desk measures about __2__ feet long.
Was your estimate close?

Find each object in your classroom.
Estimate. Then measure the length using a ruler.

1.

Estimate. about _____ feet long

Measure. about _____ feet long

2.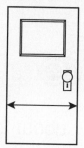

Estimate. about _____ feet long

Measure. about _____ feet long

Estimating and Measuring with Feet

Find each object in your classroom.

Estimate the length or height.

Then measure using a ruler.

	Estimate.	Measure.
1.	about _____ feet	about _____ feet
2.	about _____ feet	about _____ feet
3.	about _____ feet	about _____ feet

Problem Solving *Reasonableness*

4. About how long might each object be?
   Circle the better estimate.

about 3 inches   about 3 feet

about 2 inches   about 2 feet

5. Draw a box around the shorter object.

Estimating and Measuring with Centimeters

This is 1 centimeter high.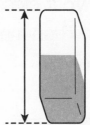

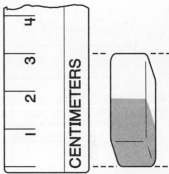

About how many centimeters high is this eraser?

The eraser is about __2__ centimeters high.
Use a centimeter ruler to measure the eraser.

When you measure height, you measure up and down.

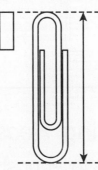

The eraser measures __3__ centimeters.
The estimate is close.

Estimate the height. Then measure using a centimeter ruler.

1.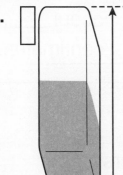

Estimate.

about _____ centimeters

Measure.

about _____ centimeters

2.

Estimate.

about _____ centimeters

Measure.

about _____ centimeters

3.

Estimate.

about _____ centimeters

Measure.

about _____ centimeters

4.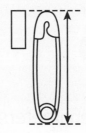

Estimate.

about _____ centimeters

Measure.

about _____ centimeters

Name _____

Estimating and Measuring with Centimeters

Find each object in your classroom.
Estimate the length. Then measure
using a centimeter ruler.

	Estimate.	Measure.
1.	about _____ centimeters	about _____ centimeters
2.	about _____ centimeters	about _____ centimeters
3.	about _____ centimeters	about _____ centimeters

Problem Solving *Reasonableness*

Are these objects taller or shorter than 10 centimeters?
Circle the better choice.

4.

taller than 10 centimeters

shorter than 10 centimeters

5.

taller than 10 centimeters

shorter than 10 centimeters

Understanding Perimeter

Count the inches around a shape to find the perimeter.

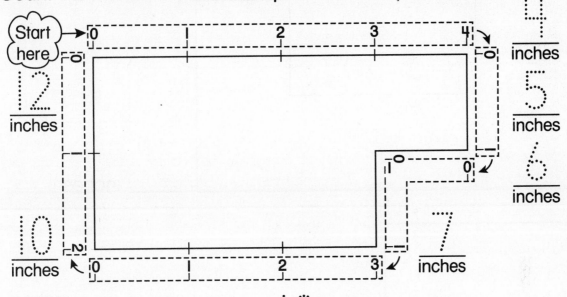

The perimeter of the shape is __12__ inches.

How many inches around each shape?

1.

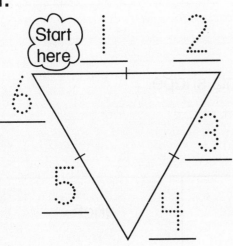

The perimeter
of the triangle is _____ inches.

2.

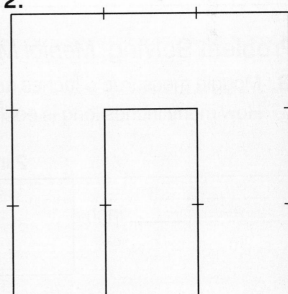

The perimeter
of the shape is _____ inches.

Understanding Perimeter

Count how many inches around each shape.

I.

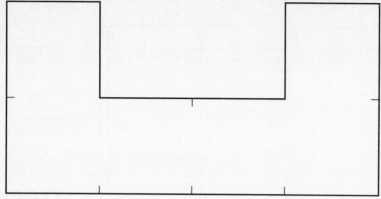

____ inches

2.

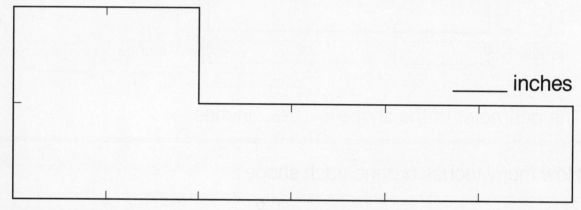

____ inches

Problem Solving *Mental Math*

3. Maggie measured 6 inches around this shape.
   How many inches long is each side?

2 inches

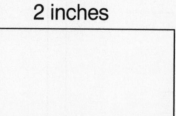

____ inch   ____ inch

____ inches

Look Back and Check

How many triangle pattern blocks will cover this shape?
Check your answers to be sure they make sense.

Mai says 4 triangle
pattern blocks will
cover this shape.

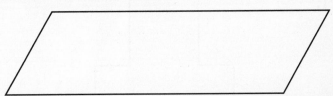

Does her answer make sense?

Check. Put triangle blocks
over the shape.

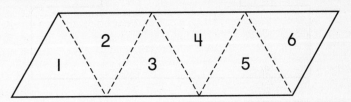

Circle the answer that makes sense.

4 pattern blocks   (6 pattern blocks)

How many triangle pattern blocks will cover each shape?
Circle the answer that makes sense.

1.

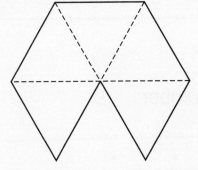

(5 pattern blocks)

8 pattern blocks

2.

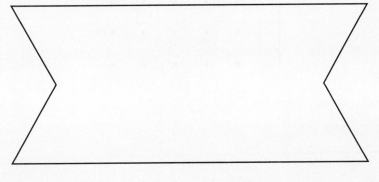

10 pattern blocks

14 pattern blocks

Name _____

Look Back and Check

How many cubes will cover each shape?
Circle the answer that makes sense.

1.

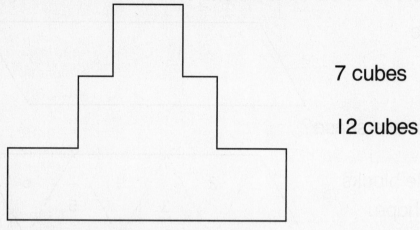

7 cubes

12 cubes

2.

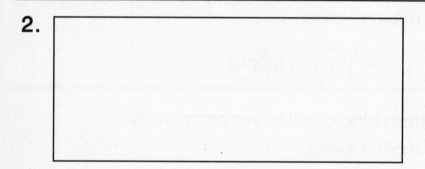

8 cubes

10 cubes

Problem Solving *Visual Thinking*

3. Draw a different shape with the same number
of square units.

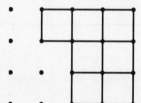   

© Pearson Education, Inc. 1

Estimating, Measuring, and Comparing Capacity

This holds 1 cup of rice.

This object holds about 2 cups of rice.

About how many cups of rice will this object hold?

Estimate.

About how many cups of rice will fill this object?

Think: How many cups will it hold.

about 5 cups

Measure.

How many cups of rice will fill the object?

Fill it with rice to measure.

about 6 cups

Estimate how many cups of rice will fill each object.
Circle your estimate. Then measure.

1.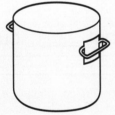

Estimate.
about 4 cups

(about 12 cups)

Measure. about _____ cups

2.

Estimate.
about 3 cups

about 7 cups

Measure. about _____ cups

Problem Solving *Estimation*

3. Circle the container that holds about 5 cups.

Estimating, Measuring, and Comparing Capacity

Estimate how many cups of rice will fill each item.
Then measure.

	Estimate.	Measure.
1.	about _____ cups	about _____ cups
2.	about _____ cups	about _____ cups
3.	about _____ cups	about _____ cups
4.	about _____ cups	about _____ cups

Problem Solving *Estimation*

5. Circle the container that holds about 2 cups.

Cups, Pints, and Quarts

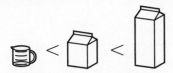

Estimate. How much milk will fill the pitcher?

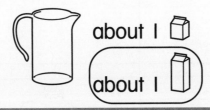

about 1 🥛

about 1 📦

Circle the best estimate.

1.

about 1

about 1

2.

about 1 🥛

about 1 📦

3.

more than 1 🥛

less than 1 🥛

4.

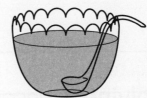

more than 1 📦

less than 1 📦

Name _____

Cups, Pints, and Quarts

Circle the best estimate.

1.  (more than I pint)

less than I pint

2.  more than I cup

less than I cup

3.  more than I cup

less than I cup

4.  more than I quart

less than I quart

5.  more than I pint

less than I pint

6.  more than I cup

less than I cup

Problem Solving *Reasoning*

Fill in each blank.

7. I pint = 2 cups

2 pints = _____ cups

8. I quart = 2 pints

2 quarts = _____ pints

© Pearson Education, Inc. 1

Use with Lesson 10-9. **123**

Liters

Estimate how much each real object will hold when filled.

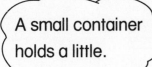

A small container holds a little.

A large container holds a lot.

| Less than a liter | About a liter | More than a liter |

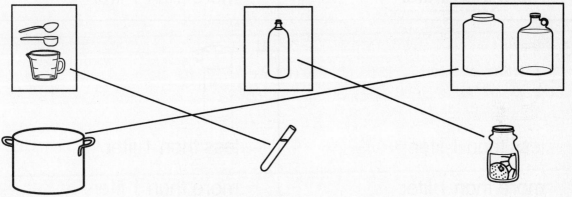

Draw a line to the best estimate.

1.

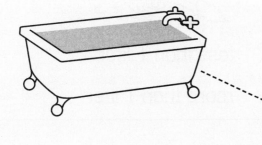

less than 1 liter

more than 1 liter

---

2.   less than 1 liter

more than 1 liter

3.      less than 1 liter

more than 1 liter

Liters

Circle the best estimate.

1.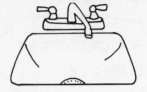

less than 1 liter

(more than 1 liter)

2.

less than 1 liter

more than 1 liter

3.

less than 1 liter

more than 1 liter

4.

less than 1 liter

more than 1 liter

5.

less than 1 liter

more than 1 liter

6.

less than 1 liter

more than 1 liter

Problem Solving *Estimation*

Circle the best estimate.

7.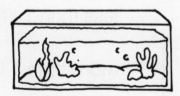

1 liter

10 liters

8.

1 liter

10 liters

Estimating, Measuring, and Comparing Weight

Does not balance.	Balances.	Does not balance.
	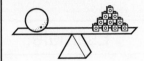	
The orange is heavier than 2 cubes.	9 cubes are as heavy as the orange.	20 cubes are heavier than the orange.

Estimate how many cubes it will take to balance.
Then measure.

1.

Estimate.

about _____ 🔲

Measure.

about _____ 🔲

2.

Estimate.

about _____ 🔲

Measure.

about _____ 🔲

3.

Estimate.

about _____ 🔲

Measure.

about _____ 🔲

4.

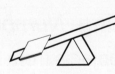

Estimate.

about _____ 🔲

Measure.

about _____ 🔲

Estimating, Measuring, and Comparing Weight

Estimate how many cubes it will take to balance.
Then measure.

		Estimate.	Measure.
I.		about _____ 🔲	about _____ 🔲
2.		about _____ 🔲	about _____ 🔲
3.		about _____ 🔲	about _____ 🔲

Problem Solving *Number Sense*

4. Number the objects from lightest to heaviest.
   Use **I** for the lightest and **4** for the heaviest.

_____ _____ _____ _____

Pounds

This weight is 1 pound.

The light bulb weighs less than 1 pound.

The melon weighs about 1 pound.

The dog weighs more than 1 pound.

Circle the best estimate.

1.

less than 1 pound

more than 1 pound

2.

less than 1 pound

more than 1 pound

3.

less than 1 pound

more than 1 pound

Pounds

Circle the best estimate.

1. less than I pound

(more than I pound)

2. less than I pound

more than I pound

3. less than I pound

more than I pound

4. less than I pound

more than I pound

5. less than I pound

more than I pound

6. less than I pound

more than I pound

7. less than I pound

more than I pound

8. less than I pound

more than I pound

Problem Solving *Mental Math*

Count by I0s to solve.

9. The class buys 8 pounds of apples.
Each pound costs I0¢.

How much does the class pay? _____ ¢

Grams and Kilograms

This feather measures about 1 gram.
1 gram is lighter than 1 kilogram.

This book measures about 1 kilogram.
1 kilogram is heavier than 1 gram.

Circle the best estimate.

1.

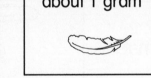
about 1 gram

about 1 kilogram

2.

about 1 gram

about 1 kilogram

3.

about 1 gram

about 1 kilogram

Name _____

Grams and Kilograms

Circle the best estimate.

1.  (grams)

   kilograms

2.  grams

   kilograms

3.  grams

   kilograms

4.  grams

   kilograms

5.  grams

   kilograms

6.  grams

   kilograms

7.  grams

   kilograms

8.  grams

   kilograms

Problem Solving *Algebra*

Solve.

9. Cindy has two puppies.

   Together they measure 7 kilograms.

   One puppy measures 3 kilograms.

   How much does the other puppy measure?

   3 + _____ = 7 kilograms

© Pearson Education, Inc. 1

Use with Lesson 10-13. **127**

Measuring Temperature

The colored part of a thermometer
measures the temperature.
It tells how hot or how cold it is.

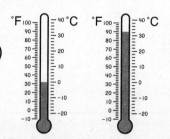

Not much of the colored
part means cold.

A lot of the colored
part means hot.

Circle the thermometer that shows the temperature.

1.

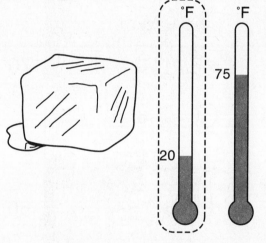

°F   °F
      75
20

2.

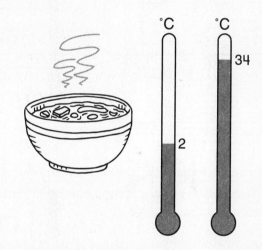

°C   °C
      34
      2

3.

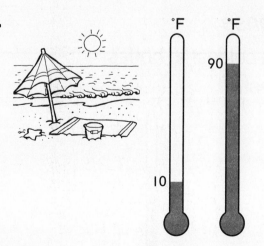

°F   °F
      90
10

4.

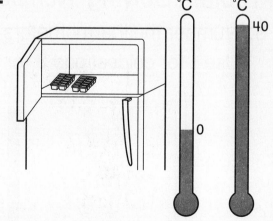

°C   °C
      40
      0

Measuring Temperature

Circle the thermometer that shows the temperature.

1.

28°F 80°F

2.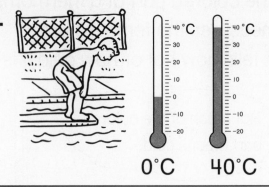

0°C 40°C

Draw lines to match each picture to the temperature.

3.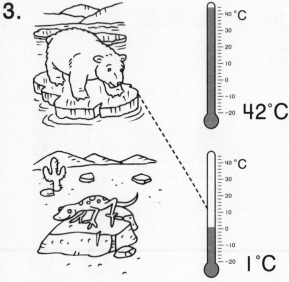

42°C

1°C

4.

70°F

50°F

Problem Solving *Number Sense*

5. Number the thermometers from coldest to hottest.
Use **1** for coldest and **3** for hottest.

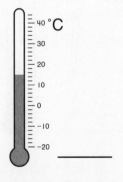

Choosing a Measurement Tool

  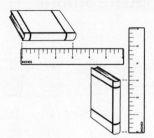

| A thermometer measures how hot or cold it is. | A ruler measures how long or how tall an object is. | A scale measures how heavy an object is. | A measuring cup measures how much something can hold. |

Circle the best tool to use for the measurement.

1. How heavy is it?

2. How long is it?

 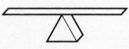 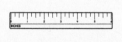

3. How hot is it?

  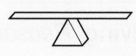

4. How much will it hold?

 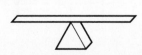 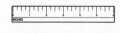

Choosing a Measurement Tool

Circle the best tool to use for the measurement.

1. How hot is it?

2. How long is it?

3. How much will it hold?

4. How heavy is it?

Problem Solving *Reasoning*

Draw something you could measure with each tool.

5.

6.

Certain or Impossible

This spinner has only 3s on it.

This spinner has no 3s on it.

I am certain to land on a 3.

It is impossible for me to land on 3.

Are you certain to land on 4 or is it impossible?

1. 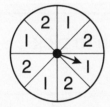　　certain

　　(impossible)

2. 　　certain

　　impossible

Are you certain to land on black or is it impossible?

3. 　　certain

　　impossible

4. 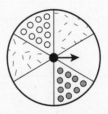　　certain

　　impossible

Color the cubes so that the sentence is true.

5. It is impossible to pick a red cube.

Certain or Impossible

Color the cubes so that each sentence is true.

1. You are certain to pick a blue cube.

2. It is impossible to pick a red cube.

3. It is impossible to pick a green cube.

4. You are certain to pick a yellow cube.

Problem Solving *Visual Thinking*

5. Draw 5 cubes in the bag. Color the cubes so that it is impossible to pick a blue cube **and** you are certain to pick a red cube.

More Likely or Less Likely

There are more gray cubes in the bag than there are white cubes.

Pick a cube. Make a tally mark. Put the cube back in the bag. Pick another cube. Make a tally mark. Put the cube back in the bag.

Color	Tally
Gray	||
White	

Since there are more gray cubes in the bag, it is more likely you will pick gray.

Fill a bag with 10 blue and 3 red cubes.
Pick a cube. Mark a tally for your pick.
Put the cube back. Do this 10 times.
Mark a tally for each pick.

1.

Color	Tally
Blue	
Red	

2. **Predict:** Which color cube is it more likely you will pick next?

_____

More Likely or Less Likely

Use each tally chart to answer the questions.

1.

Color	Tally
Black	IIII
White	IIII III

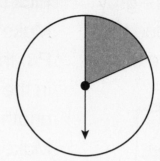

Predict:

On which color is the spinner
more likely to land on next? _____

2.

Color	Tally
Black	IIII I
White	IIII IIII II

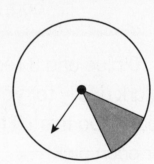

Predict:

On which color is the spinner
less likely to land on next? _____

Problem Solving *Algebra*

Solve.

3. Tony spun this spinner 12 times.
He landed on white 3 times.
How many times did he
land on black?

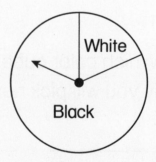

____

Name _____

Stir-Fry It!

Japanese chopsticks are shorter than Chinese chopsticks. Japanese chopsticks are about 8 inches long. Is 8 inches more than 2 centimeters or less than 2 centimeters?

more than 2 centimeters

Check your answer.
Use your centimeter ruler to show 2 centimeters. Use your inch ruler to show 8 inches.

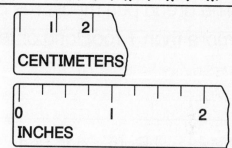

Does your answer make sense?

yes

I don't need to show all 8 inches.
2 inches is longer than 2 centimeters.

1. Jerry wants to make a pair of chopsticks.
   The chopsticks will be 8 inches long.
   The wood Jerry will use is 1 foot long.
   Is 8 inches more than a foot or less than a foot?

   _____

2. The wood cost 35¢. Jerry gave the clerk a quarter and 2 nickels. Did he get change? _____

Writing in Math

3. Ask the children in your class if they have ever eaten with chopsticks. Make a tally chart to show their answers.

Name _____

Stir-Fry It!

Read each exercise. Solve.

1. Raffi and his dad are making bread. Raffi measures 1 cup of milk. Is 1 cup more than 1 pint or less than 1 pint?

   _____

2. The bread pan measures 8 inches. Is the bread pan more than 1 foot long or less than 1 foot long?

   _____

3. What will Raffi's dad use to measure how hot the oven is? Circle your answer.

   _____

4. It takes a half hour to make chow mein. It takes 2 hours to make bread. Which takes longer to make?

   _____

5. Raffi wants to have milk to drink with his bread. Will he have more than 1 liter or less than 1 liter?

   _____

Writing in Math

6. Ask 10 children in your class if they prefer bagels or muffins. Make a tally chart to show their answers.

Name _____

Doubles

When you add the same number to itself, you are using doubles.

◇   1
◇ + 1
‾‾‾
2

◇◇   2
◇◇ + 2
‾‾‾
4

◇◇◇   3
◇◇◇ + 3
‾‾‾
6

◇◇◇◇   4
◇◇◇◇ + 4
‾‾‾
8

Use doubles to add. Draw doubles to help you.

1. ◇◇◇◇◇   5
◇◇◇◇◇ + 5
‾‾‾
10

2. ○○○○○○   6
             + 6
‾‾‾

3. ○○○○○○○   7
             + 7
‾‾‾

4. ○○○○○○○○   8
              + 8
‾‾‾

Problem Solving *Visual Thinking*

5. For each picture write an addition sentence
that tells how many buttons there are.

__2__ + ____ = ____   ____ + ____ = ____

Name _____

Doubles

Circle the doubles. Then add.

1.
   5   6   6   8   5   2
  + 5   + 7   + 3   + 8   + 8   + 2
  ____   ____   ____   ____   ____   ____

2.
   4   2   7   8   4   5
  + 2   + 7   + 7   + 1   + 4   + 2
  ____   ____   ____   ____   ____   ____

3.
   7   5   3   6   9   4
  + 1   + 0   + 3   + 9   + 2   + 4
  ____   ____   ____   ____   ____   ____

4.
   6   5   6   9   5   1
  + 6   + 7   + 8   + 9   + 4   + 1
  ____   ____   ____   ____   ____   ____

Problem Solving *Visual Thinking*

5. For each picture write an addition sentence
   that tells how many fingers are showing in all.

___ + ___ = ___   ___ + ___ = ___

Doubles Plus 1 and Doubles Minus 1

You can use a doubles fact to help you add one more
or one less.

| | Add 1 more to 4 + 4. | Take 1 away from 4 + 4. |

$$\begin{array}{r} 4 \\ + 4 \\ \hline 8 \end{array}$$

$$\begin{array}{r} 4 \\ + 5 \\ \hline 9 \end{array}$$

$$\begin{array}{r} 4 \\ + 3 \\ \hline 7 \end{array}$$

Add 1 more or take 1 away from each doubles fact.

1.
$$\begin{array}{r} 3 \\ + 3 \\ \hline 6 \end{array}$$

$$\begin{array}{r} 3 \\ + 4 \\ \hline 7 \end{array}$$

$$\begin{array}{r} 3 \\ + 2 \\ \hline 5 \end{array}$$

2.
$$\begin{array}{r} 5 \\ + 5 \\ \hline \end{array}$$

$$\begin{array}{r} 5 \\ + 6 \\ \hline \end{array}$$

$$\begin{array}{r} 5 \\ + 4 \\ \hline \end{array}$$

3.
$$\begin{array}{r} 6 \\ + 6 \\ \hline \end{array}$$

$$\begin{array}{r} 6 \\ + 7 \\ \hline \end{array}$$

$$\begin{array}{r} 6 \\ + 5 \\ \hline \end{array}$$

Problem Solving *Mental Math*

Answer each question.

4. Don has 8 red balloons.
He has 9 yellow balloons.
How many balloons does
Don have in all?

_____ balloons

5. Kit has 5 blue balloons.
She has 4 orange balloons.
How many balloons does
Kit have in all?

_____ balloons

Doubles Plus I and Doubles Minus I

Add the doubles.

Then use the doubles to help you add.

I.

Think

$5 + 5 =$ ___10___

so $5 + 6 =$ ___11___

and $5 + 4 =$ ___9___

2.

Think

$3 + 3 =$ _____

so $3 + 4 =$ _____

and $3 + 2 =$ _____

3.

Think

$7 + 7 =$ _____

so $7 + 8 =$ _____

and $7 + 6 =$ _____

4.

Think

$8 + 8 =$ _____

so $8 + 9 =$ _____

and $8 + 7 =$ _____

Problem Solving *Mental Math*

Answer each question.

5. Paco has 5 model cars. He gets 6 more cars for his birthday. How many cars does he have now?

_____ model cars

6. Lynn picks 5 tulips. She picks 4 daisies. How many flowers did she pick in all?

_____ flowers

Adding 10

You can use tens to add.

This is one group of 10.

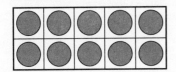

This is 10 and 1 more.

This is 10 and 3 more.

10

10 + 1 = 11

10 + 3 = 13

Draw counters. Then find the sum.

1.

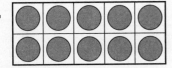

10 + 5 = 15

2.

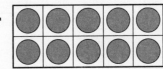

10 + 6 = _____

3.

10 + 7 = _____

4.

10 + 4 = _____

5.

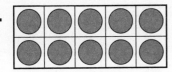

10 + 9 = _____

6.

10 + 8 = _____

Name _____

Adding 10

Draw the counters. Then find the sum.

1.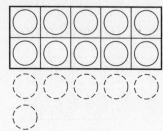

10 + 6 = _____

2.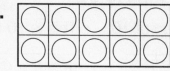

10 + 4 = _____

Write the addition problem for each ten-frame.

3.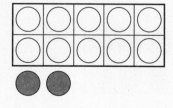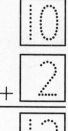

4.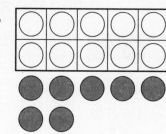

5.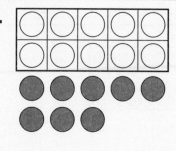

6.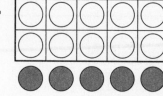

Problem Solving *Algebra*

7. Find the pattern. Then write the missing numbers.

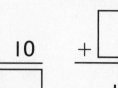

4	5	☐	7	☐	9
+ 10	+ ☐	+ 10	+ ☐	+ 10	+ ☐
☐	15	16	17	18	☐

Making 10 to Add

Making 10 can help you add.

Add 7 + 4. Make a 10.

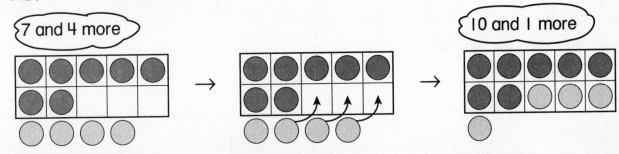

So 7 + 4 and 10 + 1 have the same sum.

7 + 4 = _____ and 10 + 1 = _____

Use counters and Workmat 2.

Draw the counters. Then write the sums.

1.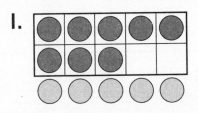

$$\begin{array}{r} 8 \\ + 5 \\ \hline 13 \end{array}$$

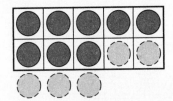

$$\begin{array}{r} 10 \\ + 3 \\ \hline 13 \end{array}$$

2.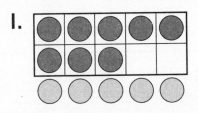

$$\begin{array}{r} 9 \\ + 6 \\ \hline \end{array}$$

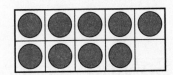

$$\begin{array}{r} 10 \\ + 5 \\ \hline \end{array}$$

3.

$$\begin{array}{r} 7 \\ + 6 \\ \hline \end{array}$$

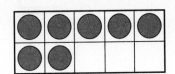

$$\begin{array}{r} 10 \\ + 3 \\ \hline \end{array}$$

Making 10 to Add

Draw the counters. Then write the sums.
Use counters and Workmat 2 if you like.

1.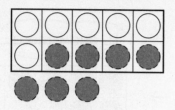

$$\begin{array}{r} 6 \\ + 7 \\ \hline 13 \end{array}$$
$$\begin{array}{r} 10 \\ + 3 \\ \hline 13 \end{array}$$

2.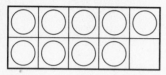

$$\begin{array}{r} 9 \\ + 5 \\ \hline \end{array}$$
$$\begin{array}{r} 10 \\ + 4 \\ \hline \end{array}$$

3.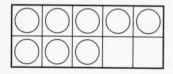

$$\begin{array}{r} 8 \\ + 3 \\ \hline \end{array}$$
$$\begin{array}{r} 10 \\ + 1 \\ \hline \end{array}$$

4.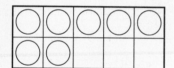

$$\begin{array}{r} 7 \\ + 5 \\ \hline \end{array}$$
$$\begin{array}{r} 10 \\ + 2 \\ \hline \end{array}$$

Problem Solving *Algebra*

Complete each number sentence.

5. $7 + 6 = 10 + 3 = \boxed{}$

6. $8 + 7 = 10 + 5 = \boxed{}$

7. $9 + 9 = 10 + 8 = \boxed{}$

Applying Addition Fact Strategies

$$\begin{array}{r} 6 \\ +\ 5 \\ \hline \end{array}$$

6 + 5 is close to 6 + 6. I can use doubles minus 1 to add.

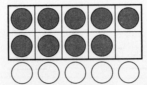

$$\begin{array}{r} 6 \\ +\ 6 \\ \hline 12 \end{array}$$

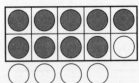

$$\begin{array}{r} 6 \\ +\ 5 \\ \hline 11 \end{array}$$

$$\begin{array}{r} 9 \\ +\ 5 \\ \hline \end{array}$$

9 is close to 10. I can make a 10.

$$\begin{array}{r} 9 \\ +\ 5 \\ \hline 14 \end{array}$$

$$\begin{array}{r} 10 \\ +\ 4 \\ \hline 14 \end{array}$$

Add. Then circle the strategy you used.

1.
$$\begin{array}{r} 8 \\ +\ 3 \\ \hline 11 \end{array}$$

doubles

(make a ten)

Think: 8 is close to 10.

2.
$$\begin{array}{r} 5 \\ +\ 4 \\ \hline \end{array}$$

doubles

make a ten

Think: 5 + 4 is close to 5 + 5. I can use doubles minus 1 to add.

3.
$$\begin{array}{r} 7 \\ +\ 5 \\ \hline \end{array}$$

doubles

make a ten

Think: 7 is close to 10. I can make a ten.

Applying Addition Fact Strategies

Add.

1.
$$\begin{array}{r} 5 \\ +9 \\ \hline \end{array} \quad \begin{array}{r} 6 \\ +7 \\ \hline \end{array} \quad \begin{array}{r} 5 \\ +6 \\ \hline \end{array} \quad \begin{array}{r} 6 \\ +8 \\ \hline \end{array} \quad \begin{array}{r} 4 \\ +8 \\ \hline \end{array} \quad \begin{array}{r} 9 \\ +7 \\ \hline \end{array}$$

2.
$$\begin{array}{r} 9 \\ +2 \\ \hline \end{array} \quad \begin{array}{r} 5 \\ +7 \\ \hline \end{array} \quad \begin{array}{r} 7 \\ +7 \\ \hline \end{array} \quad \begin{array}{r} 8 \\ +7 \\ \hline \end{array} \quad \begin{array}{r} 9 \\ +3 \\ \hline \end{array} \quad \begin{array}{r} 5 \\ +8 \\ \hline \end{array}$$

3.
$$\begin{array}{r} 7 \\ +6 \\ \hline \end{array} \quad \begin{array}{r} 8 \\ +5 \\ \hline \end{array} \quad \begin{array}{r} 3 \\ +7 \\ \hline \end{array} \quad \begin{array}{r} 6 \\ +9 \\ \hline \end{array} \quad \begin{array}{r} 9 \\ +4 \\ \hline \end{array} \quad \begin{array}{r} 4 \\ +7 \\ \hline \end{array}$$

4.
$$\begin{array}{r} 9 \\ +5 \\ \hline \end{array} \quad \begin{array}{r} 8 \\ +9 \\ \hline \end{array} \quad \begin{array}{r} 6 \\ +6 \\ \hline \end{array} \quad \begin{array}{r} 8 \\ +3 \\ \hline \end{array} \quad \begin{array}{r} 4 \\ +9 \\ \hline \end{array} \quad \begin{array}{r} 7 \\ +5 \\ \hline \end{array}$$

Problem Solving *Writing in Math*

5. Write a story problem that can be
solved by making ten to add.
Then explain how to solve the problem.

_____

_____

Adding Three Numbers

When you add three numbers, look for facts you know.
Then add the other number.

⑥
④ $6 + 4 = 10$

$+ 3$ $10 + 3 = 13$

13

The numbers are in a different order.

4
③ $3 + 6 = 9$

$+⑥$ $9 + 4 = 13$

13

The sum is the same.

Find each sum. Add the circled numbers first.
Then add the other number.

1. ⑤
2 $5 + 5 = \underline{10}$

$+⑤$ $\underline{10} + 2 = \underline{12}$

$\underline{12}$

5
② $2 + 5 = \underline{7}$

$+⑤$ $\underline{7} + 5 = \underline{12}$

$\underline{12}$

---

2. ③
⑥ $3 + 6 = \underline{\hspace{1cm}}$

$+ 4$

$\underline{\hspace{1cm}} + 4 = \underline{\hspace{1cm}}$

3
⑥ $6 + 4 = \underline{\hspace{1cm}}$

$+④$

$\underline{\hspace{1cm}} + 3 = \underline{\hspace{1cm}}$

---

3. ⑦
③ $7 + 3 = \underline{\hspace{1cm}}$

$+ 4$

$\underline{\hspace{1cm}} + 4 = \underline{\hspace{1cm}}$

7
③ $3 + 4 = \underline{\hspace{1cm}}$

$+④$

$\underline{\hspace{1cm}} + 7 = \underline{\hspace{1cm}}$

Name _____

Adding Three Numbers

Circle the two numbers you add first.
Then find the sum.

1.
 8
  3
+ 2
_____
13 |10|

  7
  4
+ 3   ☐

  9
  1
+ 5   ☐

2.
  6
  3
+ 4   ☐

  5
  5
+ 7   ☐

  2
  8
+ 7   ☐

Problem Solving *Algebra*

3. The three numbers on
each branch add up to 12.
Find the missing numbers.

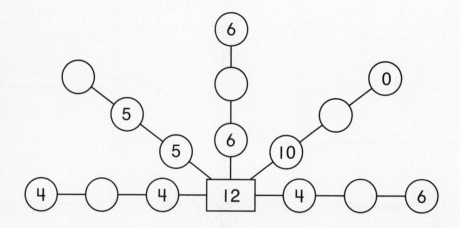

Make a Table

Jan is making groups of flowers. The flowers are red,
blue, and yellow. Each group has 3 flowers on it.
How many different groups can Jan make?

Read and Understand

You need to find how many different ways you can
put the flowers together.

Plan and Solve

You can make a table.

Count how many ways
you made.

There are _____ ways.

Look Back and Check

Did you find all the ways?
How can you check?

Red Flowers	Blue Flowers	Yellow Flowers
3	0	0
0	3	0
0	0	3
2	1	0
2	0	1

You can have 3 flowers of one color.

You can have 2 flowers of one color and 1 flower of another color.

You can have 1 flower of each color.

Make a Table

Make a table to solve the problem.

1. José is making snack packs. He has bags of raisins, nuts, and pretzels. Each snack pack has 3 bags. How many different snack packs can José make?

   There are _____ different ways.

Raisins	Nuts	Pretzels
3	0	0

Reasoning

2. What do you notice about the sum of each column of the table?

_____ _____

_____

Using Related Facts

These two facts are related.

The addition sentence and the subtraction sentence have the same 3 numbers.

$9 + 3 = 12$
$12 - 3 = 9$

The sum of the addition sentence is the first number in the subtraction sentence.

Add. Then write a related subtraction fact.

1. $8 + 4 = \underline{12}$

$\underline{12} - \underline{4} = \underline{8}$

2. $7 + \underline{6} = \underline{13}$

$\underline{13} - \underline{6} = \underline{}$

3. $9 + 2 = \underline{}$

$\underline{} - 9 = \underline{}$

4. $8 + 5 = \underline{}$

$\underline{} - 8 = \underline{}$

5. $9 + 7 = \underline{}$

$\underline{} - 9 = \underline{}$

6. $8 + 7 = \underline{}$

$\underline{} - 8 = \underline{}$

Name _____

Using Related Facts

Write related addition and subtraction
facts for each picture.

1.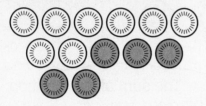

$$8 + 5 = 13$$

$$13 - 5 = 8$$

2.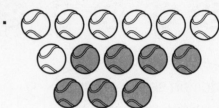

____ + ____ = ____

____ − ____ = ____

3.

____ + ____ = ____

____ − ____ = ____

4.

____ + ____ = ____

____ − ____ = ____

Problem Solving *Number Sense*

Write two related facts to answer the questions.

5. There are 7 blue balloons and 8 red balloons.

How many balloons are there in all?   ____ + ____ = ____

If 8 balloons break,
how many balloons are left now?   ____ − ____ = ____

Fact Families

This is a fact family.

$8 + 4 = 12$

$4 + 8 = 12$

$12 - 8 = 4$

$12 - 4 = 8$

Each number sentence has the same 3 numbers.

Complete each fact family. Use counters to help you.

1. | 6 | 11 | 5 |

$6 + 5 = \underline{11}$

$5 + \underline{6} = 11$

$11 - 5 = \underline{6}$

$11 - \underline{6} = 5$

2. | 9 | 5 | 14 |

$9 + 5 = \underline{\hspace{1cm}}$

$5 + \underline{\hspace{1cm}} = 14$

$14 - 5 = \underline{\hspace{1cm}}$

$14 - \underline{\hspace{1cm}} = 5$

3. | 7 | 6 | 13 |

$7 + 6 = \underline{\hspace{1cm}}$

$6 + \underline{\hspace{1cm}} = 13$

$13 - 6 = \underline{\hspace{1cm}}$

$13 - \underline{\hspace{1cm}} = 6$

Fact Families

Complete each fact family.

1.

$6 + 7 = $ _____

____ $+$ ____ $=$ ____

$13 - 7 = $ _____

____ $-$ ____ $=$ ____

Use the numbers on each fish to write a fact family.

2.

____ $+$ ____ $=$ ____

____ $+$ ____ $=$ ____

____ $-$ ____ $=$ ____

____ $-$ ____ $=$ ____

3.

____ $+$ ____ $=$ ____

____ $+$ ____ $=$ ____

____ $-$ ____ $=$ ____

____ $-$ ____ $=$ ____

Problem Solving *Algebra*

Write the missing number for each fact family.

4. 15 _____ 9

5. 5 13 _____

Using Addition to Subtract

$6 + 5 = 11$

$11 - 5 = \underline{6}$

You can use an addition fact to help you write a subtraction fact with the same numbers.

Add. Then use the addition fact to help you subtract.
Use cubes if you like.

1.

$4 + 9 = \underline{13}$

$13 - 9 = \underline{4}$

2.

$8 + 7 = \underline{}$

$15 - 7 = \underline{}$

3.

$7 + 4 = \underline{}$

$11 - 4 = \underline{}$

4.

$6 + 7 = \underline{}$

$13 - 7 = \underline{}$

Using Addition to Subtract

Circle the addition fact that will help you subtract. Then subtract.

1. $12 - 5 = \underline{7}$

   $(5 + 7 = 12)$

   $5 + 6 = 11$

2. $17 - 9 = \underline{}$

   $9 + 7 = 16$

   $8 + 9 = 17$

3. $11 - 4 = \underline{}$

   $4 + 6 = 10$

   $4 + 7 = 11$

4. $13 - 8 = \underline{}$

   $5 + 9 = 14$

   $8 + 5 = 13$

5. $16 - 8 = \underline{}$

   $8 + 8 = 16$

   $8 + 9 = 17$

6. $15 - 6 = \underline{}$

   $6 + 10 = 16$

   $9 + 6 = 15$

Problem Solving *Mental Math*

Solve.

7. Roger does 8 of his 15 math problems.
   How many problems does Roger still need to do?

   _____ problems

Using 10 to Subtract

Subtract 13 − 7.

	Cross out 7.	What is left?	

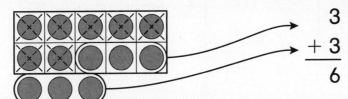

13
− 7

3
+ 3
6

13
− 7
6

Cross out to subtract. Use counters if you like.

1. 11
− 8

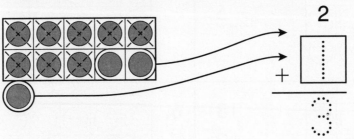

2
+
3

11
− 8

---

2. 17
− 9

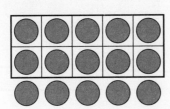

1
+

17
− 9

---

3. 15
− 7

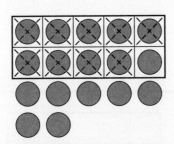

15
− 7

---

4. 16
− 8

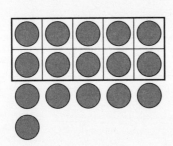

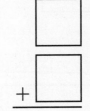

16
− 8

Using 10 to Subtract

Cross out to subtract.

Use a ten-frame and counters if you like.

1. 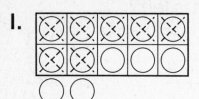 $\begin{array}{r} 12 \\ -\ 7 \\ \hline \end{array}$ 5

2. 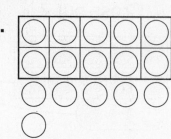 $\begin{array}{r} 16 \\ -\ 9 \\ \hline \end{array}$

3. 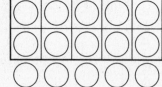 $\begin{array}{r} 15 \\ -\ 6 \\ \hline \end{array}$

4. 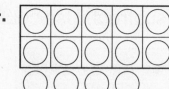 $\begin{array}{r} 14 \\ -\ 7 \\ \hline \end{array}$

5. 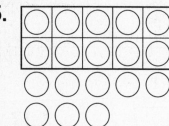 $\begin{array}{r} 18 \\ -\ 9 \\ \hline \end{array}$

6. 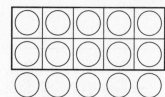 $\begin{array}{r} 15 \\ -\ 7 \\ \hline \end{array}$

7. 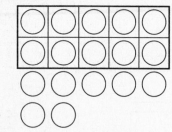 $\begin{array}{r} 17 \\ -\ 9 \\ \hline \end{array}$

8. 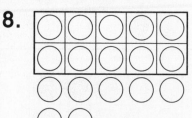 $\begin{array}{r} 17 \\ -\ 8 \\ \hline \end{array}$

Problem Solving *Estimation*

Circle your answer.

9. You bought some juice.
   You gave the clerk a dime
   and a few nickels. How much
   did the juice probably cost?

 12¢   14¢   25¢

Applying Subtraction Fact Strategies

14
− 9
_____

I know that 9 + 5 = 14. I can use the related fact to find 14 − 9.

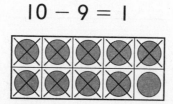

9 ○○○○○○○○○
+ 5 ●●●●●
_____
14

14 ⬛⬛⬛⬛⬛⬛⬛⬛⬛○○○○○
− 9
_____
5

14
− 9
_____

I can use 10 to subtract.

10 − 9 = 1   1 + 4 = 5

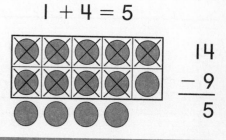

14
− 9
_____
5

Subtract.

Then circle the strategy you used.

1.   13
        − 7
        _____
        6

(7 + 6 = 13)   use a related fact

(10 − 7 = 3
  3 + 3 = 6)   use 10

---

2.   14
        − 6   use a related fact

                     use 10

3.   12
        − 5   use a related fact

                     use 10

---

4.   15
        − 6   use a related fact

                     use 10

5.   17
        − 9   use a related fact

                     use 10

Applying Subtraction Fact Strategies

Subtract.

1.
$$\begin{array}{r} 14 \\ -\ 9 \\ \hline \end{array}\qquad \begin{array}{r} 13 \\ -\ 5 \\ \hline \end{array}\qquad \begin{array}{r} 15 \\ -\ 7 \\ \hline \end{array}\qquad \begin{array}{r} 16 \\ -\ 8 \\ \hline \end{array}\qquad \begin{array}{r} 11 \\ -\ 8 \\ \hline \end{array}\qquad \begin{array}{r} 12 \\ -\ 7 \\ \hline \end{array}$$

2.
$$\begin{array}{r} 18 \\ -\ 9 \\ \hline \end{array}\qquad \begin{array}{r} 15 \\ -\ 6 \\ \hline \end{array}\qquad \begin{array}{r} 14 \\ -\ 5 \\ \hline \end{array}\qquad \begin{array}{r} 16 \\ -\ 9 \\ \hline \end{array}\qquad \begin{array}{r} 11 \\ -\ 3 \\ \hline \end{array}\qquad \begin{array}{r} 15 \\ -\ 8 \\ \hline \end{array}$$

3.
$$\begin{array}{r} 17 \\ -\ 8 \\ \hline \end{array}\qquad \begin{array}{r} 12 \\ -\ 5 \\ \hline \end{array}\qquad \begin{array}{r} 13 \\ -\ 7 \\ \hline \end{array}\qquad \begin{array}{r} 16 \\ -\ 7 \\ \hline \end{array}\qquad \begin{array}{r} 12 \\ -\ 4 \\ \hline \end{array}\qquad \begin{array}{r} 14 \\ -\ 7 \\ \hline \end{array}$$

4.
$$\begin{array}{r} 10 \\ -\ 5 \\ \hline \end{array}\qquad \begin{array}{r} 13 \\ -\ 9 \\ \hline \end{array}\qquad \begin{array}{r} 14 \\ -\ 6 \\ \hline \end{array}\qquad \begin{array}{r} 17 \\ -\ 9 \\ \hline \end{array}\qquad \begin{array}{r} 14 \\ -\ 8 \\ \hline \end{array}\qquad \begin{array}{r} 11 \\ -\ 5 \\ \hline \end{array}$$

Problem Solving *Reasonableness*

Circle your answer.

5. If Mary has 13 − 8 pennies and
   Terry has 13 − 6 pennies, then
   which sentence is true?

   Mary has more pennies than Terry.

   Terry has more pennies than Mary.

Multiple-Step Problems

Jill has 6 marbles. She gets 5 more.
How many marbles does she have in all?

$6 + 5 = \underline{11}$ marbles

Think: I know Jill has 11 marbles in all. I know she gives 8 to Sal. I can subtract to find how many she has left.

Jill gives 8 marbles to Sal.
Now how many marbles
does Jill have?

$11 - 8 = \underline{3}$ Jill has $\underline{3}$ marbles left.

Solve each problem.

1. Jack has 4 model cars. He gets 3 more model cars.
   How many model cars does Jack have in all?

   $\underline{3} + \underline{4} = \underline{7}$ model cars

   For his birthday Jack gets 5 model cars.
   How many model cars does he have now?

   _____ + _____ = _____ model cars

2. Nicky has 6 charms on her bracelet. She buys 8 more.
   How many charms does Nicky have in all?

   _____ + _____ = _____ charms

   On the way home 4 charms are lost.
   How many charms does Nicky have now?

   _____ − _____ = _____ charms

Name _____

PROBLEM-SOLVING SKILL

Multiple-Step Problems

Solve each problem.

1. Jan read 14 books this month.

   6 books were about horses.

   The rest were mysteries.

   How many books were mysteries?

   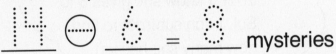 mysteries

   Jan plans to read 4 more mysteries.

   How many mysteries will she have read in all?

   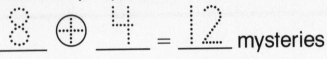 mysteries

2. Peter read 7 dinosaur books.

   He read 8 books about sharks.

   How many books did Peter read in all?

   _____ ◯ _____ = _____ books

   Of all the books he read,
   there were 6 that Peter didn't like.

   How many books did he like?

   _____ ◯ _____ = _____ books

© Pearson Education, Inc. 1

On the Farm

There are 12 hens in a barnyard.

4 hens are brown. The rest are white.

How many hens are white?

$12 - 4 =$ _8_

Use a related addition fact to check your answer.

$4 + 8 =$ _12_   So, $12 - 4 =$ _8_.

---

1. 4 cows are in the barn.   4
   7 cows are in the pen.   7
   3 cows are in the meadow. $+\ 3$
   How many cows are there in all?   _____ cows

---

2. The farmer has 17 baskets   <u>Check</u>
   of strawberries.   17
   He sells 9 baskets. $-\ 9$ $+$
   How many baskets are left?   _____ 17   _____ baskets

Writing in Math

3. Draw a picture of 14 eggs. Write a
   subtraction story about your picture.
   Then write a number sentence.

   _____

   _____

   _____ $-$ _____ $=$ _____

Name _____

On the Farm

Solve.

1. There are 8 eggs in one nest.
   There are 7 eggs in another nest.
   How many eggs are there in all?

   _____ ◯ _____ = _____ eggs

   Kendra is collecting the eggs.
   Her basket holds 10 eggs.
   How many eggs will be left in the nests?

   _____ ◯ _____ = _____ eggs

2. There are 7 white hens. There are 5 brown hens.
   There are 3 hens that are gray.
   How many hens are there in all?

   _____ + _____ + _____ = _____ hens

3. Circle the strategy you used to solve Exercise 2.
   make a ten   use doubles

Writing in Math

4. Draw a picture of 13 eggs. Write a subtraction story about your
   picture. Then write a number sentence to go with your story.

   _____ ◯ _____ = _____

Adding Groups of 10

You can use what you know about adding ones
to add groups of ten.

2 ones and 5 ones are 7 ones.   2 tens and 5 tens are 7 tens.

$$2 + 5 = 7 \qquad 20 + 50 = 70$$

Write each number sentence.

1.

$$\underline{3} + \underline{2} = \underline{5} \qquad \underline{30} + \underline{20} = \underline{50}$$

2.

$$\underline{} + \underline{} = \underline{6} \qquad \underline{} + \underline{} = \underline{60}$$

3.

$$\underline{} + \underline{} = \underline{} \qquad \underline{} + \underline{} = \underline{}$$

4.

$$\underline{} + \underline{} = \underline{}$$

5.

$$\underline{} + \underline{} = \underline{}$$

Adding Groups of 10

Write each number sentence.

1.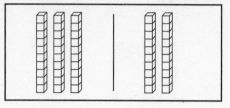

   <u>30</u> + <u>20</u> = <u>50</u>

2.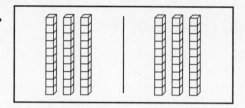

   _____ + _____ = _____

3.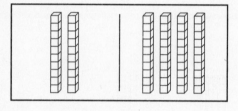

   _____ + _____ = _____

4.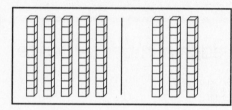

   _____ + _____ = _____

Write each sum.

5. 50 + 20 = _____   30 + 40 = _____   20 + 20 = _____

6. 70 + 20 = _____   60 + 30 = _____   10 + 80 = _____

Problem Solving *Number Sense*

Circle the two groups that answer the riddle.

7. David has two books of stamps. He has more than
   60 stamps. Which are David's stamp books?

Stamps of
the U.S.A.   Stamps of France   Stamps of Japan   Stamps of Mexico

40   20   10   30

Adding Tens to Two-Digit Numbers

You can count on by tens to add.

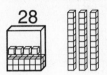

3 tens

10   10   10

28 + 30 is 28 + 3 tens   28, __38__ , __48__ , __58__

28 + 30 = 58

Solve each number sentence.

1. 31

10   10   10   10   10

31, __4I__ , __5I__ , __6I__ , __7I__ , __8I__

31 + 50 is 31 + __5__ tens

31 + 50 = __8I__

2. 52

52 + 20 is 52 + _____ tens   52, _____ , _____

52 + 20 = _____

3. 33

33 + 40 is 33 + _____ tens   33, _____ , _____ , _____ , _____

33 + 40 = _____

Adding Tens to Two-Digit Numbers

Write each number sentence.

1.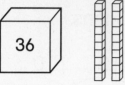

$$\underline{36} + \underline{20} = \underline{56}$$

2.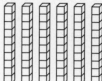

_____ + _____ = _____

3.

_____ + _____ = _____

4.

_____ + _____ = _____

5.

_____ + _____ = _____

6.

_____ + _____ = _____

Problem Solving *Algebra*

7. Write the missing numbers. Then write the next addition problem in the pattern.

37	47	57	☐	☐
+ 10	+ ☐	+ 10	+ 10	+ ☐
☐	57	☐	77	☐

Adding Two-Digit Numbers

Find the sum of 25 and 13.

Add the ones.

Add the tens.

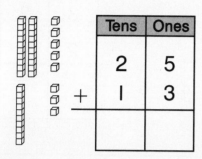
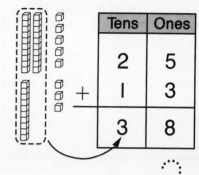

Tens	Ones
2	5
1	3

Tens	Ones
2	5
1	3
	8

Tens	Ones
2	5
1	3
3	8

$5 + 3 = \underline{8}$

$2 + 1 = \underline{3}$

$25 + 13 = \underline{38}$

$20 + 10 = \underline{30}$

Draw and add the ones and tens. Find each sum.

1. Find the sum of 43 and 24.

Add the ones.

Add the tens.

Tens	Ones
+	

Tens	Ones
+	

Tens	Ones
+	

_____ + _____ = _____

_____ + _____ = _____

$43 + 24 = \underline{}$

_____ + _____ = _____

Adding Two-Digit Numbers

Write each sum.

1.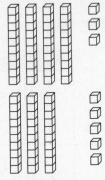

Tens	Ones
4	3
+ 3	5
7	8

2.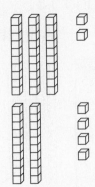

Tens	Ones
3	2
+ 2	4

3.

Tens	Ones
1	7
+ 6	1

Tens	Ones
6	3
+ 2	3

Tens	Ones
4	3
+ 5	2

Tens	Ones
5	3
+ 2	5

4.

Tens	Ones
3	5
+ 4	3

Tens	Ones
5	6
+ 3	1

Tens	Ones
4	3
+ 2	1

Tens	Ones
2	6
+ 2	2

Problem Solving *Reasoning*

Circle the number that solves each riddle.

5. I am less than 47 + 10.
I have fewer tens than ones.
Which number am I?

57   37   42

6. I am greater than 15 + 23.
I have more ones than tens.
Which number am I?

37   45   55

© Pearson Education, Inc. 1

Regrouping in Addition

Add 26 and 5.

Show 26.	Add 5.	Regroup 10 ones as 1 ten.

Tens	Ones		Tens	Ones		Tens	Ones		Tens	Ones

$26 + 5 = \underline{31}$

Find the sum.

1. Add 16 and 7.

Show 16.	Add 7.	Regroup.	Find the sum.

Tens	Ones		Tens	Ones		Tens	Ones		Tens	Ones

$16 + 7 = \underline{23}$

---

2. Add 28 and 5.

Show 28.	Add 5.	Regroup.	Find the sum.

Tens	Ones		Tens	Ones		Tens	Ones		Tens	Ones

$28 + 5 = \underline{\hspace{1cm}}$

Name _____

Regrouping in Addition

Use cubes and Workmat 4. Circle **yes** or **no**.
Then write the sum.

	Show	Add	Do you need to regroup?		Find the sum.
1.	27	6	(yes)	no	$27 + 6 =$ 33
2.	43	5	yes	no	$43 + 5 =$ _____
3.	34	8	yes	no	$34 + 8 =$ _____
4.	17	4	yes	no	$17 + 4 =$ _____
5.	56	3	yes	no	$56 + 3 =$ _____
6.	93	2	yes	no	$93 + 2 =$ _____
7.	87	7	yes	no	$87 + 7 =$ _____
8.	68	5	yes	no	$68 + 5 =$ _____

Problem Solving *Number Sense*

Use the number line to add.

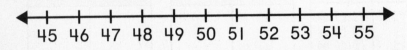

45 46 47 48 49 50 51 52 53 54 55

9. $47 + 6 =$ _____

10. $49 + 1 =$ _____

11. $46 + 3 =$ _____

12. $48 + 5 =$ _____

PROBLEM-SOLVING SKILL   **R 12-5**

Exact Answer or Estimate?

Al has 2 bags of name tags.

Each bag has 12 name tags.

There are 18 children in his group.

Does he have enough name tags for all of the children?

Read and Understand

You need to know if 2 bags of name tags

are enough for 18 children.

Do you need an exact answer or an estimate?

Plan and Solve

12 is more than 10, so 12 + 12 is greater than 10 + 10.

18 is less than 10 + 10. You can estimate that there are enough.

exact answer   (estimate)

Look Back and Check

Does your answer make sense?

Is an exact answer or an estimate needed

to solve each problem?

Circle **exact answer** or **estimate.**

1. Jody wants to buy 4 stickers.
   They cost 7¢ each. Jody
   has 45¢. Does she have
   enough money?

   exact answer   estimate

2. Jody has 12 stickers.
   She has 3 pages left in her
   sticker book. Can she put
   4 stickers on each page?

   exact answer   estimate

Exact Answer or Estimate?

Circle **exact answer** or **estimate**.

1. Lizzie is making curtains.

   Each window is 36 inches wide.

   There are 2 windows.

   How much cloth should Lizzie buy?

   Do we need an exact answer or an estimate?

   exact answer   estimate

2. Don wants to buy peaches. They cost 50¢.

   Don has 2 quarters, a dime, and a nickel.

   Does he have enough money?

   Do we need an exact answer or an estimate?

   exact answer   estimate

3. Eric has 6 packs of trading cards.

   Each pack has 8 trading cards.

   He wants to give one trading card to each child in his class.

   There are 20 children in his class.

   Does he have enough cards?

   Do we need an exact answer or an estimate?

   exact answer   estimate

Problem Solving *Estimation*

Circle the better estimate.

4. About how many grapes can you eat?

   about 10   about 100

5. How many quarters can you hold in your hand?

   about 5   about 50

Subtracting Groups of 10

Subtracting groups of 10 is like subtracting ones.

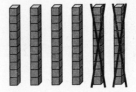

6 − 2 = __4__

60 − 20 = __40__

Complete each number sentence.

1.

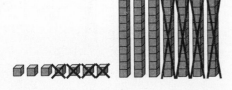

5 − 1 = __4__   50 − 10 = __40__

2.

6 − 3 = _____   60 − 30 = _____

3.

7 − 4 = _____   70 − 40 = _____

4.

5 − 4 = _____   50 − 40 = _____

Problem Solving *Mental Math*

Solve.

5. A star sticker and a sun sticker cost 50¢ altogether. The star sticker costs 20¢ by itself. How much does the sun sticker cost?

 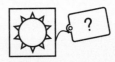

_____¢

Subtracting Groups of 10

Write each number sentence.

1.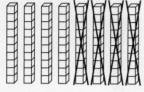

$$\underset{}{80} - \underset{}{40} = \underset{}{40}$$

2.

_____ − _____ = _____

3.

_____ − _____ = _____

4.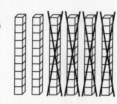

_____ − _____ = _____

5.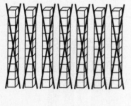

_____ − _____ = _____

6.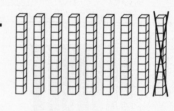

_____ − _____ = _____

Problem Solving *Mental Math*

Solve.

7. Meg spends 70¢ on a pencil case and ruler.
The pencil case was 40¢.
How much did the ruler cost?

_____¢

Subtracting Tens from Two-Digit Numbers

You can count back by tens to subtract.

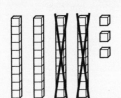

2 tens

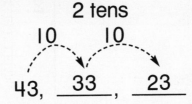

43, __33__ , __23__

43 − 20 is 43 − 2 tens

43 − 20 = __23__

Solve each number sentence.

I.

10

34, __24__

34 − 10 is 34 − __1__ ten

34 − 10 = __24__

2.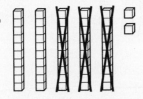

10

52, ____, ____, ____

52 − 30 is 52 − ____ tens

52 − 30 = ____

3.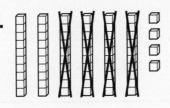

64, ____, ____, ____, ____

64 − 40 is 64 − ____ tens

64 − 40 = ____

Name _____

Subtracting Tens from Two-Digit Numbers

Write each number sentence.

1.

   $\underline{6^4} - \underline{2^0} = \underline{44}$

2.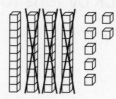

   _____ − _____ = _____

3.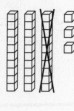

   _____ − _____ = _____

4.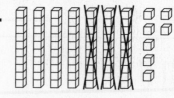

   _____ − _____ = _____

5.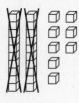

   _____ − _____ = _____

6.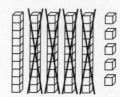

   _____ − _____ = _____

Problem Solving *Reasonableness*

7. Robert says that 75 − 30 = 35.
   Is he correct? Explain.

   _____

   _____

Subtracting Two-Digit Numbers

Find the difference for 38 − 16.

Subtract
the ones.

Subtract
the tens.

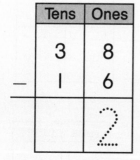

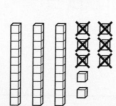

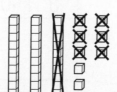

Tens	Ones
3	8
− 1	6
	2

Tens	Ones
3	8
− 1	6
2	2

Write each difference.

1.

Subtract
the ones.

Subtract
the tens.

Tens	Ones
4	6
− 3	2

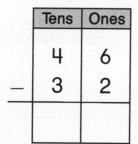

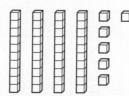

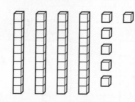

Tens	Ones
4	6
− 3	2

2.

Subtract
the ones.

Subtract
the tens.

Tens	Ones
5	8
− 2	5

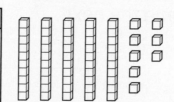

Tens	Ones
5	8
− 2	5

Subtracting Two-Digit Numbers

Write each difference.

1.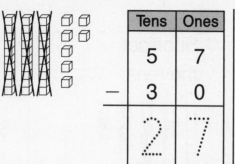

Tens	Ones
5	7
− 3	0
2	7

2.

Tens	Ones
4	8
− 2	4

3.

Tens	Ones
5	8
− 3	3

Tens	Ones
8	7
− 5	3

Tens	Ones
5	6
− 2	4

Tens	Ones
3	4
− 1	4

4.

Tens	Ones
7	5
− 4	3

Tens	Ones
6	4
− 2	2

Tens	Ones
3	2
− 3	2

Tens	Ones
9	6
− 5	4

Problem Solving *Algebra*

Write the missing numbers. Then write the next
subtraction sentence in the pattern.

5.

$$87 \qquad 77 \qquad 67 \qquad \square \qquad \square$$

$$- 10 \qquad - \square \qquad - 10 \qquad - 10 \qquad - \square$$

$$\square \qquad 67 \qquad \square \qquad 47 \qquad \square$$

Regrouping In Subtraction

Find the difference for the problem 32 − 6.

Show 32.

Regroup 1 ten as 10 ones.

Subtract.

Tens	Ones

Tens	Ones

Tens	Ones

Subtract 6.

$32 − 6 = \underline{26}$

I. Find the difference for the problem 46 − 8.

Show 46.

Regroup.

Subtract.

Tens	Ones

Tens	Ones

Tens	Ones

Subtract 8.

$46 − 8 = \underline{38}$

2. Find the difference for the problem 23 − 7.

Show 23.

Regroup.

Subtract.

Tens	Ones

Tens	Ones

Tens	Ones

Subtract 7.

$23 − 7 = \underline{}$

Name _____

Regrouping in Subtraction

Use cubes and Workmat 4. Circle **yes** or **no**.
Then write the difference.

	Show	Subtract	Do you need to regroup?		Find the difference.
1.	42	6	(yes)	no	42 − 6 = _36_
2.	37	5	yes	no	37 − 5 = _____
3.	62	4	yes	no	62 − 4 = _____
4.	58	9	yes	no	58 − 9 = _____
5.	24	7	yes	no	24 − 7 = _____
6.	77	6	yes	no	77 − 6 = _____
7.	85	8	yes	no	85 − 8 = _____
8.	93	3	yes	no	93 − 3 = _____

Problem Solving *Visual Thinking*

9. Draw the missing cubes.

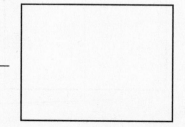

Name _____

Make a Graph

The bead store sells red, white, and blue beads.
Which color bead did they sell the most?

> Count by tens. Then count on by fives.

Beads Sold				
	Week 1	Week 2	Week 3	Week 4
Red Beads	10	5	10	10
Blue Beads	10	5	5	10
White Beads	10	10	10	10

Read and Understand

The chart shows how many of each color beads were
sold. We want to find which color sold the most.

Plan and Solve

Use the information in the chart to make a graph.
Color one box for every 5 beads sold.

> Count the boxes by fives.

Beads Sold

Red Beads										
Blue Beads										
White Beads										

0   5   10   15   20   25   30   35   40   45   50
Number of Beads Sold

The _____ beads sold the most.

Look Back and Check

How can you be sure your answer is correct?

Name _____

Make a Graph

Make a graph to solve the problem.
Color one box for every 10 books.

1. The first grade classes made a chart showing
   how many books they read each day.
   Which class read the most books?

Number of Books Read

Class	Day 1	Day 2	Day 3	Day 4	Day 5
Mrs. Miller's Class	30	20	10	10	30
Mr. Lee's Class	10	30	20	10	10
Miss Plum's Class	20	20	10	20	10

Mrs. Miller's Class										
Mr. Lee's Class										
Miss Plum's Class										

    0   10   20   30   40   50   60   70   80   90   100

_____ class read the most books.

Writing in Math

2. Write another question that could
   be answered using the graph.

   _____

   _____

156 Use with Lesson 12-10.

Caring for Kittens

The Kitty-Cat Pet Shop has 23 squeaky cat toys.
The store owner buys 20 more squeaky cat toys.
How many squeaky cat toys does the pet shop
have altogether?

23 and __20__ more is how many altogether?

Use counting on by ten to add: 23 + __20__ = __43__

The pet shop has __43__ squeaky cat toys.

---

1. On Monday, the Kitty-Cat Pet Shop
   sold 10 squeaky cat toys. How many
   squeaky cat toys does the store have left?

   _____ ◯ _____ = _____ squeaky cat toys

2. Jimmy bought 5 white rubber mice
   and 4 blue rubber mice. How many
   rubber mice did he buy?

   _____ ◯ _____ = _____ rubber mice

3. Jimmy lost 2 rubber mice. How many
   rubber mice does he have left?

   _____ ◯ _____ = _____ rubber mice

PROBLEM-SOLVING APPLICATIONS

Caring for Kittens

1. Eduardo and his family went to the pet store.
   The pet store had 28 long-haired kittens and
   20 short-haired kittens. How many kittens did
   the pet store have altogether?

   _____ ◯ _____ = _____ kittens

2. Eduardo gets a long-haired kitten.
   His sister, Elena, gets a short-haired kitten.
   How many kittens does the pet store have now?

   _____ ◯ _____ = _____ kittens

3. Elena buys a toy mouse for her kitten.
   It costs 37¢. Elena has

   Will she get change? _____

Writing in Math

4. Eddie wants to buy a collar for 59¢ and a ball
   for 7¢. Does he need to regroup to find out
   how much they will cost? Explain.

   _____

   _____